"This book deserves [...] for every parent regardless of faith, color, creed, or economic status. It is a wise one-of-a-kind book that will make your child's life happier and more meaningful. *Raising Your Child to Be a Mensch* will prove to be a classic."

> Dr. Wayne Dyer, Author of
> *What Do You Really Want
> for Your Children*

"In a time when many Americans are wondering about our lost sense of ethics and morals, Rabbi Kurshan dares to write about such things as values and God. We can all learn from this wonderful book the lesson: 'happiness comes from doing the right and good thing.' This is important reading for parents of young children."

> Dennis Wholey, Author of
> *The Courage to Change*

"All parents who love their children must read this book."

> Harvey Ruben, M.D.
> Associate Professor of Clinical
> Psychology, Yale University

"I have an inexhaustible number of Catholic married nieces and nephews I'm going to give this book to, so that I can look forward to dozens of grandniece and grandnephew mensches."

> John Cardinal O'Connor,
> Archbishop of New York

RAISING YOUR CHILD TO BE A MENSCH

Neil Kurshan

IVY BOOKS • NEW YORK

Ivy Books
Published by Ballantine Books
Copyright © 1987 by Neil Kurshan

All rights reserved under International and Pan-American Copyright Conventions. Published in the United States by Ballantine Books, a division of Random House, Inc., New York, and simultaneously in Canada by Random House of Canada Limited, Toronto.

No part of this book may be reproduced or transmitted in any form or by any means, electronic or mechanical, including photocopying, recording or by any information storage and retrieval system, without permission in writing from the Publisher.

Library of Congress Catalog Card Number: 85-48149

ISBN 0-8041-0377-1

This edition published by arrangement with Atheneum Publishers, an imprint of Macmillan Publishing Company.

Manufactured in the United States of America

First Ballantine Books Edition: March 1989

*To my wife, Alisa,
and my children, Ilana,
Naamit, Ariella,
and Eytan,
who have always forgiven
me when I have failed
to be a mensch.*

When I was young, I admired
clever people. Now that I am old,
I admire kind people.
        —ABRAHAM JOSHUA
            HESCHEL

Contents

Acknowledgments

I began this book with little understanding of the time and discipline required to transform a deeply held ideal into a book. I am grateful to my literary agents, Arthur and Richard Pine, who never let my disclaimers that I was not a writer stand as the final word. Without their persistence and confidence in me I would not have undertaken this project.

Many thanks to my talented editor, Susan Ginsburg, who always cushioned the bad news with the good and did not let me rest until the final manuscript. A special note of thanks to Tom Cowan who helped me rethink, restitch, and rewrite the early draft.

I also thank the many friends and family members who read this book at various stages and candidly shared their suggestions with me. I am also indebted to the members of my present congregation in Huntington, New York, and to the members of the congregations I have previously served. Their lives have been intertwined with mine and their experiences are a part of this book. In recounting their stories I have changed names, dates, and circumstances to protect the confidentiality which is a *sine qua non* of our relationship with each other.

And a special word of appreciation to my wife, Alisa, my toughest and most loving critic. Her patience and understanding have reminded me that I am a very fortunate man.

Introduction:
No Prizes for Being Nice

> *He has told you, O man, what is good,*
> *And what the Lord requires of you:*
> *Only to do justice,*
> *And to love goodness,*
> *And to walk modestly with your God.*
> —MICAH 6:8

I am certain about the kind of people I want my children to become. I am less certain—in fact, I am worried—about the pressures working against them.

Recently a young mother in my congregation shared with me an incident that sums up the problem that haunts me. Her twelve-year-old daughter, a very capable, conscientious child who does well in school, came home in tears one day after an awards ceremony and blurted out, "Mommy, why don't they hand out prizes for just being nice?" Her mother echoed her daughter's question to me, "Rabbi, why doesn't anyone encourage the qualities we love the most in our daughter? How can we raise her to be generous and sensitive to other people when no one else seems to care?"

These questions are the questions of this book. In a world filled with pressures to achieve, to excel, to become number one, and to look out for only number one, how can we raise children who will work hard to get ahead without losing their capacity to be decent and kind? In a world where there are no prizes for being nice, how do we raise children who will care about being good? In a society that stresses looking out for yourself and fulfilling your own desires, how can we teach children to be concerned for others and to work toward a common good?

I have a feeling that our parents and grandparents found these questions less troubling. In an era of more widely shared values and fewer alternative lifestyles from which to choose, they had more confidence in their ability to raise children. Perhaps in knowing less they were more certain of what they knew. Those who led lives of hard work, long hours, and poverty could not indulge themselves or their children. They knew that they wanted their children to enjoy a better life than they had, and by necessity this goal was etched into the pattern of their daily lives. They did not have to lecture or sermonize about responsibility or concern for others. They were living examples of it.

A few generations ago when Jewish parents spoke of compassion, decency, and fairness they called it "mensch-lichkeit." My own parents wanted me to grow up and achieve many worthwhile goals, but it would all be meaningless, they told me, if I did not also become a mensch. My parents and their parents did not live in a world of saints. They lived in a world with its share of callous and unscrupulous people, but they were convinced there was a right way and a wrong way of doing things. They expected us to learn the right way. Although they lived in difficult times, in many ways less hospitable than our own, they were convinced that with honesty and hard work it could be a better world for us.

We are more tentative in our assumptions as parents. Many of us have gone to college and been deluged by all the conflicting theories of human behavior. We have taken the social and developmental psychology courses, and we have read the handbooks. We know the Mayan Indians wrapped their infants in hammocks and left them suspended alone in darkness for many hours of the day without any dire effects. We also know about Harlow's baby monkeys who were deprived of the love and attention of their mothers and had difficulty relating to other monkeys. We read about Native Americans who disciplined their children without resorting to physical punishment.

Like Hamlet, we can see both sides—sometimes many sides—to every issue, and we are stymied by indecisiveness and inaction. To stay or not to stay at home with the children is an issue for which each side can marshall compelling evidence. An increasing number of child care experts suggest that we are sacrificing our child's well-being if we immediately return to work and leave them with someone else. At the same time, we are told that we will be better parents if we are successful in our careers and don't view our children as obstacles to advancement.

We know too many conflicting approaches to childrearing to be certain that there is only one right way of raising children. We have been exposed to too many different lifestyles to be sure that there is only one acceptable pattern of life or only one right set of values. We know too much about the complexity of human behavior to believe that our children will conform exactly to our expectations. Our lack of certainty makes us vulnerable to all the conflicting advice about how to be a good parent. Is it any wonder we are anxious, worried, or doubtful that we have what it takes?

When I became a father, I realized very quickly that the childrearing handbooks do not always help. Like many first-time parents, I read all the books during my wife Alisa's pregnancy, and by the time Ilana was born I had a high pile beside the bed. When they arrived home from the hospital, I nervously faced a three-day-old baby girl hoping the stack of books that was bigger than she was would help. They did not. After a few sleepless nights for her and for us, our baby daughter taught us our first lesson about childrearing: she would not conform to a stack of books.

When there has been a specific problem, the more helpful books have reassured us that our children will recover from their illnesses, that they will learn to walk, and that they will be able to read. For that reassurance I am indebted to the doctors, psychologists, educators, and other experts whose thoughtful, commonsense books were available when we needed them.

A decade ago I could have written a childrearing guide with clear and explicit rules. I had no children then. Now I feel like the young psychologist who began his career on the lecture circuit with a talk entitled "The Ten Commandments for Parents." He married and became a father. The lecture title became "Ten Hints for Parents." After the birth of his second child he retitled his lecture "A Few Suggestions for Parents." When his third child was born he stopped lecturing.

As the father of four children, I cannot write a cookbook filled with recipes for producing a good child. My wife and I have learned—often the hard way through our own mistakes—that each of our children is an exception to the rules by which we thought they would grow. What works for one does not work for the others. What works in one situation does not work in another. Sometimes there are simply no easy answers to a difficult family situation.

I remember a family I had come to know during my first few years with a congregation. They were a typical family with a hardworking father, a mother who was the mainstay of the family, three teenage children, and a grandmother who also lived in the house. You couldn't find a more tightly knit, loving family. Then suddenly the mother became seriously ill and without warning died a few months later. The grandmother, a strong figure herself, stepped into the breach but died of a broken heart exactly a year after her daughter's death. I watched the family decline rapidly. The father had to work long hours to support the children and could not be both father and mother. The oldest daughter dropped out of college, the middle child started drinking and staying out late at night, and the youngest son became involved with drugs and eventually ended up in a residential treatment center. What had once been a happy household disintegrated before my eyes, and neither I nor the family's friends had any simple solutions for preventing it.

Even when circumstances are within our control, holding a family together and raising good children is a tough job. We need to be compassionate while remaining firm, able to identify with our children while serving as an adult model for them, steadfast in our standards but forgiving when they fall short. With hard work and a measure of luck, it can be done. I must confess, nonetheless, that sometimes I feel like all four of the women in an old joke who got together for lunch. One commented, "Oy." The second sighed, "Oy vay." The third added, "Oy vay iz mir." At this point the fourth woman jumped in and said, "I thought we agreed not to talk about our children."

There are no shortcuts to good parenting. The satisfactions from children are some of the deepest life can offer, but they are only achieved with a lot of hard work and love, and a large dose of luck. While I have a fundamental confidence that, God willing, my children will find their own distinctive paths through childhood and adolescence, I am not sure at this point exactly how they will go about it. I only know that there will be wonderful times when they will make Alisa and me happy and proud to be their parents, and other moments when they will cause us to ask ourselves if we have failed.

We all want the best for our children. We want them to develop their talents and reach their full potential. We hope we will avoid the mistakes our own parents made and eliminate the obstacles we had to overcome. Our natural desire to give our children every possible advantage makes us highly susceptible to every claim, theory, and fad that promises to be in our children's best interests. When our neighbors enroll their tots in gymnastics, swimming, reading, and music programs, we ask ourselves if we are depriving our children by not enrolling them as well. If we do not know the latest theory of childrearing or send our children to the most prestigious school, we worry that we are imposing a handicap on them which they will have to overcome later in life.

A director of an information center about private schools in New York City commented that some parents are so worried about good nursery schools that she gets calls from mothers in the hospital who have just delivered! Other parents enroll their four- and five-year-olds in tutorial programs designed to coach them for the standardized admission tests required to get into most private nursery schools! Clearly something is wrong when these kinds of parental anxieties dominate the first few years of a new child's life and crowd out the more basic pleasures of just being with the child and trusting our natural instincts to love and nurture the baby.

In this welter of programs and opportunities, we can so easily forget our dreams about the kind of people we want our children to become. If we get so absorbed in good schools, good grades, and good jobs before a child can even walk, how easily we can forget that the fundamental good in anyone's life is to be a good person.

One of my former pupils who is now a premedical student went to the reserve reading room of his college library to do the reading for his organic chemistry exam. He took the first book off the shelf and found that the assigned pages had been cleanly sheared from the book with a razor blade. He went to the next book. Again the assigned pages were missing. In each book with assigned readings for the exam, the pages had been removed. What kind of future doctor would remove class materials either to use for himself or to prevent classmates from completing the reading? Would we want this doctor, however brilliant, to treat us or our children? Would he or she be more preoccupied with career, wealth, and advancement than our welfare and our lives?

7

There are no simple prescriptions or magical formulas for raising a mensch. There is no curriculum, set of exercises, or bottle of time-released tablets to provide our children with the proper dosage of menschlichkeit at every stage of their lives. This book does not contain long lists of rules, techniques, or strategies for raising a mensch. I don't think such a book could be written; I know I could not write it.

Instead I offer a book that will suggest ways of thinking about our children, about ourselves as parents, of clarifying our hopes for them, and of instilling in them an ideal toward which they can aspire. We all have expectations for our children and can offer them living examples of generosity and human kindness. I hope this book will be a reminder to you—as indeed it began as a reminder to myself—that the most important goal we can have for our sons and daughters is that they grow up to be kind, moral, and responsible human beings—in a word, that each of them grows up to be a mensch.

1. The Disappearing Mensch

What bothered me was people. Why should people be so cruel to each other, when they could be so kind? Why should human beings bring suffering to one another as well as to themselves when they could all live together in peace and good will?

—SHOLOM ALEICHEM

It is hard to raise good children. Our society places so many obstacles in the way of becoming a good person that our children often don't know to whom they can turn for support and direction. They grow up in a world that can be cruel and immoral, plagued by epidemics of vandalism and crime. They learn to fight back when other kids are mean to them. The pervasiveness of cheating in school and scandals in public life disillusion them at an early age. Their natural idealism grows cynical. Children of divorce lose trust in their own parents. Teenage suicide becomes ever more common as our young people choose the ultimate cry for help. Are we really listening to them as they try to handle—often unsuccessfully—the overwhelming pressures of growing up in such a hurry?

Children have a lot to learn—and too many sources to learn it from. Parents, teachers, religious leaders, siblings, peers, social and political leaders, the media—it's not surprising they receive mixed messages. "Win; lose graciously. Get ahead; be content with your own abilities. Look out for yourself; be your brother's keeper. Do well in school; do well at home. Get a job; develop your personality. Be tough; be good." Over and over the message seems to say, "Get it all—or there's something wrong with you."

And what are our own goals in raising our children? Do we too send them mixed messages? We would like them to be accomplished, successful, financially secure, smart, talented, well groomed, healthy and happy, to marry, and not forget to call home! These are natural wishes of normal parents. But we also have other dreams. We want our children to become warm, decent human beings who reach out generously to those in need. We hope they find values and ideals to give their lives purpose so they contribute to the world and make it a better place because they have lived in it. Intelligence, success, and high achievement are worthy goals, but they mean nothing if our children are not basically kind and loving people.

Goodness is not an innate or natural disposition. People are not born good any more than they are born evil. They are simply born male or female. They *become* human beings, capable of kindness or cruelty. The simple Yiddish expression says it all: *makhn fun kinder menschen*—making human beings out of children. Raising human beings is a process of teaching children right from wrong and turning them into responsible individuals. In traditional Jewish families a child was reminded daily, if not hourly, to eat like a mensch, dress like a mensch, talk like a mensch, and behave like a mensch. Through a loving mixture of coaxing, cajoling, crying, and commanding a child was transformed from an undisciplined creature into a mensch. Even to this day I can hear the question my parents asked me time and time again, "When will you become a mensch?" And on many occasions I still fall short of my expectations for myself. Menschlichkeit is a lifelong goal.

A friend who grew up in Boston received daily Bible lessons from his grandmother who lived with the family. A self-educated, deeply religious woman, she found teaching her grandson was an uphill struggle. He was frequently distracted by the other children playing outside, and his eyes and mind would drift out the window. Whenever the grandmother noticed his attention wandering, she would chide him gently, "David, David, you will have so much time to play ball during your life, but will you find the time to become a mensch?"

"Zay a mensch!" — *"Be a mensch!"* — was an expression repeated a thousand times in the homes of many first generation Jewish immigrants. Children who knew no other words of Yiddish knew these three words. Menschlichkeit is responsibility fused with compassion, a sense that one's own personal needs and desires are limited by the needs and desires of other people. A mensch acts with self-restraint and humility, always sensitive to the feelings and thoughts of others. As menschen we feel a genuine passion to alleviate the pain and suffering of those around us.

The term "mensch" literally means a "person" or "man," but it represents a moral ideal for all people, men and women alike. A woman can be as much a mensch as a man. Kindness and decency transcend gender. A mensch brings a sense of responsibility to every undertaking and treats everyone fairly and justly. Menschlichkeit is the opposite of cruelty, pettiness, and self-centeredness. It means being sensitive to other people's needs and seeking out ways to help them. It is acquired by living close to family and extending one's sense of obligation beyond the family to the broader community. In the Jewish culture of Eastern Europe where the term arose, to call someone a mensch was the highest compliment that could be given.

A classical illustration of menschlichkeit is the rabbi who invited several guests to his table one Friday night to usher in the Sabbath. The meal had barely begun when one of the guests became a little too excited about the point he was making in the conversation and knocked against the table, spilling his cup of red wine onto the white linen tablecloth. Seeing the pain and embarrassment of his guest, the rabbi quickly kicked the table leg near his own foot causing his own glass to topple over and spill. He then turned to his guest and apologized, "I am sorry for the miserable condition of this table. I have been intending to fix it for some time and will see to it immediately after the Sabbath."

I am reminded of this story every time I react to some trivial incident in anger rather than compassion. After a hectic day I finally sit down at the dinner table with my family for a little peace and quiet. If I am lucky I get a few tranquil moments and then suddenly one of my children will accidentally overturn a glass of ice water onto my lap or the grape juice onto the tablecloth. The other children shriek and head toward dry land. My wife goes for a towel. Unlike the rabbi who shook the table to share in his guest's embarrassment, my first instinct is to shake my child. Accusations come so easily: "What is the matter with you?

How can you be so clumsy? I have to wear these pants tonight! Don't you know that you can't get grape juice stains out of a tablecloth?" I know by the tears in the child's eyes how badly he or she feels and I know that I have only made things worse. I could just as well have said, "Don't worry. It was an accident. Let's clean it up together." But on some nights it's much easier to be angry than to be concerned about the feelings of a little child.

Menschlichkeit does not develop by itself. A six-year-old brother does not instinctively get along with his four-year-old sister. A teenager does not automatically help around the house. A parent does not always react with patience to a misbehaving child. Ultimately, the right thing to do is not always clear and is not simply a matter of common sense—either to children or adults.

Children do not magically learn morality, kindness, and decency any more than they magically learn math, English, or science. They mature into decent and responsible people by emulating adults who are examples and models for them, especially courageous parents with principles and values who stand up for what they believe.

It is not always easy to stand firm in our beliefs. A few years ago a woman was driving beside me on the highway with two children in the back seat of her car. As far as I was concerned she and I were going at the right speed, but apparently it was too slow for the man behind her. He impatiently raised his finger at her in an obscene gesture. When she did not speed up, he shouted vulgarities at her from his car. At the first red traffic light this little lady, who must have been no more than 5′2″ tall, stormed out of her car and confronted the man, a muscular six-footer who would have towered over her if he had gotten out. But the feisty woman leaned against his door and told him in no uncertain terms that if he ever repeated his actions in front of her or her children she would take him to court. He didn't get out of his car.

I doubt that this woman carefully thought through what she did. She might never have said anything if she had considered all the possible consequences of talking back to such a brute. She was simply fed up and decided she would not let herself be the victim of abuse in front of her children. She acted from impulse, but it was impulse grounded in a sense of fairness and decency.

Sometimes our children themselves recognize injustice and come to the rescue. Jeff, the son of some friends of ours, rode a school bus with children going to a variety of schools, including one Jewish youngster from a Hasidic family. The other children teased the poor boy mercilessly. No one would sit with him. They made fun of his traditional side curls and simple white shirt and black pants. They accused him of sleeping with hair curlers like a girl and of having only one set of clothes. Each day the boy was reduced to tears. After several days of this, Jeff got on the bus and sat down beside the Hasidic boy, announcing: "Don't pay attention to them. They are just saying stupid things. I'll sit with you." From that day until the end of the year the two boys sat together and became friends.

It is understandable that when adults no longer respect one another, children will no longer respect each other or adults. One of my neighbors began her career as an English teacher. She is a bright, idealistic person who had dreamed for many years of inspiring high school students to read and love literature as she does. When her own children reached school age, she found a job in a good suburban school system. On the first day of school her students stole from her purse, put gum between the pages of her roll book, and sabotaged her pen so that it squirted ink in her face. Within two weeks she gave up teaching, disillusioned and unhappy. I often wonder how other teachers in situations like hers can continue to go into the classroom year after year when students feel they have a right to talk back and challenge all authority. In some school districts teachers even live with an ever present fear of physical attack. It seems that the older, safer world in which being a good, decent, and responsible person was a measure of one's life has disappeared. So many of our children are growing up without a clear sense of right and wrong.

I once asked a man who was a generous contributor to many causes how he had become such an enthusiastic benefactor. He attributed his generosity to his grandmother. "When I was a child," he told me, "my family would often spend the weekend at my grandmother's apartment. She lived simply on the small amount of money my grandfather left her when he died, rarely spending anything on herself. In her kitchen closet she had a pushka, a coinbox for charity. Each Friday at sunset before lighting the candles she would take the box off the shelf and put a quarter in it. As I grew older I would ask her why she didn't save those quarters to buy a little something for herself. Her answer was always the same. 'God has been good to me; He has given me a good life and a wonderful family. I save up those quarters to give to people who are less fortunate.' To me that quarter from my grandmother is like a thousand dollars. Whenever I give, I still see her dropping a quarter in the pushka."

You can't be a good role model for your children if you

fear them. Over the years I have met couples who hide five or ten dollars in their dresser for their children to find because they fear their kids will otherwise steal a lot more from their purse. I know parents who do not set a curfew because they fear their children will ignore them and parents who bite their tongues when their children call them "morons" or "idiots" to their face. Fear of a child is the first step toward raising an immoral tyrant. If your children sense that you feel powerless toward them, they will step into the vacuum and rule dictatorially. A teenager I know was unhappy with his summer job at camp and called home after the first week to get out of his job. He demanded that his mother call the camp and concoct a story that his father was having emergency open-heart surgery and needed the boy at his side. The mother obligingly made the call and told the lie just as her son had dictated.

No one says that raising good children is easy. Sometimes it's difficult to stand up for our beliefs and set the right examples for our young ones. Too often I let an unacceptable remark pass or compromise my ideals. Yet I'm sure we all can proudly recall moments when we stood our ground—when a younger child threw a tantrum to play with a neighbor's child who was a bad influence, when we refused to let an older child go to an unsupervised party where there would be drugs or alcohol, or when we insisted that our son or daughter not give up a babysitting commitment at the last minute because of an invitation to do something more fun.

We want our children to be compassionate and decent, to have fun and yet show responsibility, to be adventurous and yet cautious, to evaluate their actions and choose with care. In other words, we want them to become menschen.

But our society provides little support or encouragement to be a mensch. Even the word mensch has faded from our vocabulary. From time to time we may hear a passing reference, but not usually in the context of childrearing. Recently I found the following ad under "Personals" in the classified section of a magazine: "Petite, thirty, West Coast female wishes to meet a mensch." I wish her luck!

By and large the word has vanished from our speech. I once asked a class of tenth-grade students to define the term. Puzzled expressions crossed their faces. Suddenly a boy's hand shot up boldly from the back of the room. I called upon the young man who had a gleam in his eye. "A mensch is a pretty woman who likes to flirt with men," he announced proudly. He seemed put off when I told him that was not what it meant. Both of us seemed confused. Later in the day it dawned on me. Wench! He had confused the term with wench!

The disappearance of the word mensch is only a symptom. More important is the disappearance of kindness, decency, and responsibility from our personal lives. Many of us have been the victims of obscene words or gestures from other drivers on the road even though we gave them virtually no provocation. We seldom hear the words "please," "thank you," or "excuse me." Locker room language is now heard in living rooms. People have no respect for anyone's feelings other than their own. Rudeness has become chic.

We pay a terrible price for the loss of menschlichkeit. The emotional fabric of our lives wears thin. Rabbi Sidney Greenberg, who has written for a Philadelphia newspaper for many years, claims that the column that drew the largest avalanche of letters from readers was the column entitled "Warm Fuzzies," a term he learned one day when his six-year-old granddaughter returned home from school and announced: "We made warm fuzzies in class today!" He asked her what a warm fuzzy might be, and she hesitated for a moment, groping for words her grandfather would understand.

"Warm fuzzies are things you say that make other people feel good." Looking in her school bag she pulled out some of the warm fuzzies she had received: "You are my best friend." "You are very pretty." "You, I like." "I like the present you gave me."

How reassuring life would be for all of us if we handed out warm fuzzies to our spouses, our children, people at work, even clerks we encounter at the bank or grocery store. We would know we are loved and appreciated. Our lives would no longer be bereft of warmth and kindness. We would feel good to be alive again.

You know how important it is to feel appreciated, to feel that you are a valuable part of a community, needed in your job, and recognized in the projects to which you volunteer time and energy. A "thank you" or a simple comment that you did a great job can make your day. We are never so successful or so secure to be untouched by a smile or a pat on the back. One doctor has estimated that the majority of his mentally ill patients could have been cured by human kindness. Of all the letters I receive the ones I remember and cherish the most are the warm fuzzies, those that tell me I helped somebody get through a difficult period or that I made a difference in their lives.

We all hope to encounter kindness in the many professionals with whom we deal. A boss who commends us for hard work, a doctor who is compassionate as well as competent, teachers who genuinely like our children and appreciate their unique strengths and talents—these are the people we will remember with fondness as the years go by.

As a young rabbi in my first congregation, I often visited people in the hospital. My early style of visiting the sick left a lot to be desired. I would walk into the room of a patient, hand out a book of prayers, and offer a few quick words of hope for a speedy recovery. I did most of the talking, and the person I was visiting did little more than say hello, good-by, and thank you. In time I learned they needed more than words. I still carry the book of prayers, but I rarely hand it out. I talk less and I listen more. I no longer recite the routine wishes for a fast recovery. In an institutional setting where the hospital staff routinely refers to "the gall bladder in 12-B" or the "bypass in 6-C," I try to remember that I am speaking with real people, not just patients. If they want to talk about family, I talk about family. If they want to talk books, we talk books. When they share their fears of illness and death, we talk about suffering and hope and faith in the future. And if a person wants to forget his or her problems momentarily and talk about me, I can talk for hours! It doesn't take a psychologist—and I am not one—to understand that caring about people is the first step in helping them.

I care about the people I visit. I respect them for their interests and concerns, and try to remember that they are more than gall bladders and bypasses. They are still human beings deserving of compassion and respect. When I was younger I thought I would carve out a professional reputation as a rabbi based on my theological expertise and my ability to theorize about God and the human soul. But today that means far less to me than being known as a patient rabbi who listens, offers a kind word, shoulders responsibilities for others, and—most of all—cares.

What is true outside our families is also true within them. You may find it easy to be kind and decent with outsiders, but really tough when it comes to family members with whom you are more emotionally involved. Never take kindness and decency for granted. Look beyond your family's faults and shortcomings. Certainly punish your children when you catch them doing something wrong, but be quick to catch them doing something right and praise them. Let them know you appreciate what they do well. Balance the cries of "Go to your room!" with invitations to be part of your life. Indicate that you appreciate your children's help, sensitivity, and sheer presence. We cannot just assume that there is love, trust, and deep regard for one another within our families. We have to show it in words and deeds.

A father told me that one rare Saturday night when his teenage son was home they were sitting at the kitchen table looking at old family photos, reminiscing about some of the ups and downs in the young man's life. Out of the blue the father looked at his son and said, "You know Mom and I love you a lot and wouldn't trade you for any other son in the world." The boy turned red and said nothing, but the next morning he ventured shyly, "Dad, you remember what you said last night? Well, it was sort of mushy, but— thanks for saying it."

Life should have "mushy moments" to balance the "tough moments" when we have to confront our children about their misbehavior—and discipline them. We should let our children know that they are the source of our joys, as well as frustrations. Raising a child may include the worst of times but it also contains the very best. If you are honest with yourself, you know in your heart that the worst of times would not convince you to wish you never had children. I think most of us would say that our lives have been enormously enriched because of them. They make our lives meaningful in a way that a career or wealth or reputation alone could never do. There is an expresssion in Yiddish for the joys of bringing up children: *tsu shepn nakhes fun kinder*—receiving satisfaction, joy, and pride from children.

Let your children know you love them. We do not always have to make speeches or give testimonials; those can sound rather unconvincing. Hug them, take walks with them, laugh with them every chance you get. Remember, your children are not mind-readers. In fact, most teenagers think their parents' minds are actually rather weird and give up trying to read them!

Not long ago I was with my children in a playground and I got absorbed in a conversation with another father. Each time one of his children yelled, "Look, Dad!" or "Daddy, watch me!" he would go over to the child, ask him to do it again, and say with great enthusiasm, "Hey, that's really great!" I commented on how responsive he was to his children and he explained to me, "I know I'm overly appreciative. But my own father was overly critical. He could always find something wrong with what I did. An 'A —' should have been an 'A.' Second prize was not first prize. He was always asking me why I couldn't be like so-and-so's son. I grew up thinking I never did a good job."

None of us wants to grow up thinking we're not good enough. We each long for recognition and acceptance for what we really are. We need encouragement to do our very best from warm, supportive people who love us even when we fail. Without the love and support of others, the world grows cold; people grow more insensitive to the needs of others; and the mensch within us disappears.

2. *"Life Is With People"*

> *Any beast can cry over the misfortunes of its own child. It takes a mensch to weep for others' children.*
> —SAM LEVENSON

"Food was my friend," explained a teenage girl who weighed 238 pounds. "There was no one to talk to, and I'd go to the kitchen and eat. There was nothing else to do." Teenage obesity has increased by more than 40 percent in the last two decades and one out of every five teenagers is too fat, according to a recent newspaper article entitled "Teenage Obesity Grows as More Kids Come Home to Empty Houses and TV." Adolescence is a difficult stage of life under the best of circumstances, but for young people who come home to empty houses in the afternoon, the loneliness of the teenage-years can be overwhelming. Food may be an inferior substitute for a parent's presence, but when there is no one around in whom you can confide or who can put a reassuring arm around your shoulder, food may become a more dependable companion.

A young man told me of a conversation he had in the

hospital with his father just before he died. The father, a perpetually busy man, had not spent much time with his children and the son expressed his regret that they had not shared more together. The father responded by reminding his son that he had to work long hours in order to put food on the table to feed the family. The son remained silent, but in his heart he was yearning to tell his father that he had never been as hungry for food as he had been for his father's presence.

So many young people are crying out to be noticed. Walk down the street of any city, and you can hear the silent cries of our children. A twelve-year-old parading around in heavy chains on her waist and neck, a dozen bracelets on her arm, multiple layers of blouses and shirts concealing her body, and heavy facepaint that masks her own delicate features is crying for a little attention. She is saying, "Look at me. Notice me!" And ironically, because of her outrageous garb and painted face, we do look but never see the real child underneath.

The most common complaint that psychologists hear from children is that no one listens to them. Parents are too busy, and before long children grow tired of voicing their feelings and sharing their hurts with adults who seem deaf or distracted. Eventually they stop trying.

Being there and listening attentively are the most valuable ways we can show our children the true meaning of menschlichkeit. There are moments which arise in the course of a day which will never recur. If we are absent, we miss them forever. Children do not keep office hours. When a two-year-old pushes over a friend or won't share a toy, we should be there to help smooth over hurt feelings. If a six-year-old has had a bad day in school because her classmates are teasing her, she cannot come home and share it with the television or someone she doesn't love and trust. A teenager who confesses after an hour of small talk that he is bothered because he is not popular might never have opened up if a parent could only give him a few minutes. If we are rarely around to welcome a child home from school, to sit in the kitchen and talk, or to tuck a child into bed, the significant moments of life may pass and never be retrieved.

Josh, a neighbor's boy, had a friend who recently committed suicide. Both boys were fifteen and had shared a long friendship with one another going back to their younger days of palling around together. Unfortunately, a few weeks before he took his life, the boy had beaten Josh for a spot on the high school basketball team that they had both had their hearts set on. At the time it seemed like a major loss to Josh, and he and his friend had a falling out. Under normal circumstances they would have probably patched things up and gone on as before. But the friend committed suicide. Josh returned home from school and reported the tragedy to his mother without showing a trace of emotion, as if it were just a normal school-day occurrence. Now, Josh's mother is a wise and loving parent. She knew it was unlike her son to be so callous. Later she told me, "Josh periodically announces that he doesn't need me around. But I knew that at some point he would break down. I didn't know when it would happen, but I decided to hover over him so that I would be there when the dam broke." Three days later, upon returning from school, he burst into tears and poured out the guilt he felt over having been angry at his friend for winning the spot on the team and not having had time to make things up before he died. She was there to hold and comfort him.

We are too quick to rationalize our failings as parents. We know we spend inadequate time with our children but we convince ourselves (if not them!) that it is "quality time." When I come home from a long hard day I am always ready for so-called quality time with my children, but I've noticed over the years I have three kinds of "quality time." The first I call "Split-Brain Time" because only one side of my brain is with my children. The other—and unfortunately the dominant side—composes lists of phone calls yet to be made, runs over errands to be done tomorrow, and calculates ways to fit unfinished work into the remainder of the evening after the kids go to bed.

The second type of quality time is what I call "Timed Time" and is best characterized by declarations such as, "Okay, you children have ten minutes to get in bed and fall asleep." *They* may not be tired but *I* am, and so we don't sit on the edge of the bed, tell stories, and talk over the events of the day or whatever else is in their heads.

On the really bad days I settle for the "Quality Greeting"—a brief "Hi there!" or "Sleep tight"—usually uttered from a comfortable chair, just before I drift off to sleep.

It's obvious to me, and I'm afraid to them too, that all of these patterns are "qualified time," not quality time; and yet on some nights it seems like all I can give them. We are not machines (fortunately!) who can walk in the door, switch off workday pressures, summon reserves of energy, and turn on "quality time" to play creatively with our children or listen attentively to their rehashing of the day.

The most important moments with our children cannot be scheduled into a time slot. A good relationship with a child, as with anyone, develops out of spontaneous experiences shared together, not from a few hurried hours scheduled into the evening. We cannot set aside an hour for discussion with our children and hope that it will be a time of deep encounter. The special moments of intimacy are more likely to happen while baking a cake together, or playing hide and seek, or just sitting in the waiting room of the orthodontist.

Quality is related to quantity. The more time we spend with our children, the greater the possibility that we will be together when the important moments of life occur. A relationship with a child cannot be compressed into an hour a day or one day a week. We cannot walk in the door and expect our children to share with us their sorrows and disappointments when they haven't seen us in days or weeks, nor can we always put off till the future the companionship which our children need today. We tell them, "I'm too busy," or "In a month things will slow down," but time passes quickly. The years of childhood are fleeting and brief. The other demands on our time may never let up. It seems as if our children were just born yesterday when they leave for college with whatever values and standards we have been able to instill. Even if that mythical day eventually arrives and we do have more time for them, we may be surprised to find that they have already grown up and acquired the habit born of necessity of managing without us.

The haunting lyrics of Harry Chapin's song, "Cat's in the Cradle," always come back to me when I notice myself not spending enough time with my children:

A child arrived just the other day.
He came to the world in the usual way.

But there were planes to catch and bills to pay.
He learned to walk while I was away.
He was talkin' before I knew
And as he grew he was saying:
"I'm gonna be like you, Dad.
You know I'm gonna be like you." . . .

Well my son turned ten just the other day.
He said, "Thanks for the ball, Dad, let's play.
Can you teach me to throw?"
I said, "Not today; I got alot to do—"
He said, "That's O. K." and he walked away.
He walked away, but his smile never dimmed.
It said, I'm gonna be like him, yeah.
You know, I'm gonna be like him. . . .

Well, I've long since retired and my son's moved away.
I called him up just the other day.
I said, "I'd like to see you if you don't mind."
He said he'd love to if he could find the time.
"You see, my new job is a hassle and the kids have the flu,
But it's sure nice talking to you, Dad,
It's been sure nice talking to you."
And as he hung up the phone it occurred to me
He'd grown up just like me
My boy was just like me.

©1974 Story Songs Ltd.

A psychologist told me the story of a five-year-old girl
he was treating who was having trouble sleeping at night.
The poor child led such a topsy-turvy life she could find
little to hold onto. A lack of reassuring routine was causing
part of the problem. Her father was never home from work
during the week before his daughter's bedtime. Some
nights her mother was home, and put her daughter to bed,
but on other nights she went out and left the little girl with
a babysitter. On still other nights the mother put her daughter to sleep but left for meetings later in the evening. The

daughter was never sure whom she would find at home if she woke up at night. The psychologist made a reasonable suggestion that the parents be at home more regularly at night. The parents recoiled in disbelief. "We just can't possibly do it," they explained. "We are both at crucial points in our careers and to cut back is to risk getting off track." The psychologist understood perfectly. He told me he feels similar pressures in his own profession. To advance his career as a child psychologist, he has to spend most of his time with other people's children and reduce the time he would like to spend with his own.

One of the hardest struggles for many parents is balancing families and careers. There are powerful voices telling us to invest the best years of our adult lives in our jobs if we hope to have successful careers. There are only a few weak voices reminding us that the best years of our lives are the ones in which our children are growing up into— we hope!—compassionate and responsible adults. Certainly we cannot always be at a child's side, but when he or she needs love and attention, there is rarely anyone else who can give it as genuinely and wholeheartedly. If we are not there, who comforts them when they have been the victims of another child's taunts? Who finds the only pattern of socks that matches the pink jumper? Who remembers that the slugger bat was buried under the football shins and the hockey net? Who welcomes our children home from school with a hug, a kiss, and a genuine interest in hearing about their day?

Raising a child and rising in a career both demand time and energy and few of us are the superparents who can excel at both. We can't always do it and neither will our children when they are parents. We should not mislead our children by telling them they can have everything when they grow up. It is a formula for frustration to suggest that they can have two well-behaved children, a high-powered and stimulating career, a worthy and supportive spouse (who also has a high-powered and stimulating career!), a housekeeper who is as good as a mother, a terrific marriage, and enough leisure time to preserve their sanity! The only people who "have it all" live their wondrous lives in the glossy pages of magazines and on our television and movie screens. I have never met them in real life. In fact, the ones I have met who are striving for this so-called "good life" usually end up without enough time for anything.

My wife has a sign posted on our refrigerator: "Isn't it funny that people hardly ever ask a man how he combines family and career." Balancing time is not only a problem for mothers; it is also a problem for fathers. A child needs a father as much as a mother. It is unfair that mothers are expected to manage the family while seeing to it that her own needs as well as everyone else's are met. Of course, we cannot demand that a parent sacrifice a career, but there will be times when family needs dictate a little less time at the office, not assuming every project that comes along, or not using income or promotions as the only measure of our accomplishments.

Sometimes a crisis forces us to question our priorities. When he was forty-two, Paul Tsongas, the United States Senator from Massachusetts, discovered he had a form of cancer which could be treated, but not cured. He was not in imminent danger, but the years remaining might be far fewer than he had hoped. He was faced with a painful choice of running again for office or spending what remaining time he had with his wife and three daughters. He hesitated; politics was his life. He had competed in six elections and won them all. In just ten years he had risen from the Lowell City Council to the U. S. Senate. He was a successful Congressman who got legislation passed and enjoyed favorable press coverage. He had never walked away from a tough challenge. His life had always focused on goals, never on limits. Like most of us, he had always assumed he would be around for a long time.

One night as his two-year-old daughter fell asleep in his arms, he broke down in tears. How often would he hold his daughter during the next seven years if he won reelection and returned to Washington? He realized his children were growing up without him. They had gotten used to their father being away. After a great deal of agonizing, he decided not to run and returned home to work in a law firm close to his family. Cancer did not drive him out of the Senate. Rather, love of his family lured him home. After his decision he received a letter from an old friend who wrote, "No one on his deathbed ever said, 'I wish I had spent more time on my business.'"

Let's hope we are wise enough to examine our priorities even without facing a life-threatening illness. All of us, fathers and mothers alike, have to adjust our schedules and make compromises with our careers. We all have many responsibilities in life. It may be especially difficult to find the time to spend with our children if we are the family's primary breadwinner, if we are a single parent, or if economic necessity forces us to work long hours. Yet neither divorce nor economic hardship should cause us to ignore our children. Whatever our family situation, most of us do not treat our children as patiently or sensitively as we should.

There is not a precise formula or pattern of family life that leads to menschlichkeit. There is no one balancing point between family and career which works for everyone. A young man whose father fell seriously ill remembers his mother giving up her personalized stationery business which she ran at home to go out and find a higher paying office job so she could support the family. When his father died, he remembers how bitterly angry he had been that his father's illness and death had deprived him of his mother's presence. The bitterness and anger eventually passed. More enduring has been the memory of his mother picking up the pieces of her life and supporting her family.

Sometimes illness, the seasonal nature of our jobs, economic circumstances, caring for an aging parent, or other family ties eat into our time. We have to be flexible. Different arrangements may work at different periods in our lives. The right balance when our children are under three will not be right when they are in high school. The right balance for one person will not be appropriate for another. Yet most of us, including myself, can probably find more time for our children and stop using our jobs as the excuse for not spending time with them. There is no work more important or rewarding than the work of raising children.

We should not be embarrassed or defensive if we really *like* taking care of children and want to be at home beyond the first three years of a child's life. Recently a woman attending a prestigious college went to the Dean of Students in tears. She confessed that more than anything else in life she wanted to get married and raise a family, but she was afraid to tell her roommates or even her boyfriend of her goals. Her fear was not so much that they would reject her, but that her own feelings were abnormal or sick! No one, even in our modern society, should feel like a member of a besieged minority for wanting to stay home and raise a family. But I know what the young woman must have been facing when I read the class notes in the back of my wife's alumnae magazine. I get a feeling for how isolated a young woman with traditional goals must feel. Comment after comment describes women rising in their careers. Rarely is there a wish of good luck for a woman raising her children. The message is clear: Bringing up a family is not much of an accomplishment.

I am not denying that full-time parenting can be tedious, tense, and trying. There is an allure to using our talents creatively in the world beyond our families. Not all of us can remain full-time parents to young children day after day without experiencing a lack of intellectual stimulation or a feeling that we are stagnating and that the world is passing us by. I have known many days when the pressures of the office become a welcome diversion after a few hours with my children. I love my children, but after the inevitable squabbles, epithet hurling, and property disputes, I am ready to hand back the childrearing responsibilities to my wife.

The right balance between career and family will depend upon economic situations, available opportunities, our own temperament, and the temperaments of our children. Every waking moment does not have to be spent with them. They need to learn as they grow up that we cannot be available to them all the time. At some point children must come to realize that we have our own interests and needs.

Whatever pattern we settle on, the fundamental guideline is to find adequate time for our children. If possible, during the school years, and that includes high school, at least one parent should be at home when a child is home. How secure and comforting it is to know that mom or dad is there when they walk in from school even if they normally have nothing to say about the day. My wife used to love coming home from high school and finding her mother there so that she could ignore her! Whatever their need—even rebellion!—your children need you there.

The busier we are, the more important it is to set aside specific times when our families know we are available to them and all outside intrusions are excluded. These may be meals or certain days of the week or activities we all enjoy doing together. Within our own family we set aside one day of the week, the Sabbath, when we do not answer the phone, go shopping, watch television, or go into the office. We make this day special. We shut out the many distractions that separate us from one another on the other days of the week. This day is a family day, and we spend it together in synagogue and at home.

Menschlichkeit develops gradually over the years, emerging little by little out of the countless interactions between parents and children. Only parents really care about raising children to be menschen. When I did something wrong as a child, I was constantly reminded by my parents, "We do not behave in our family this way." And only they could say those words with authority and conviction. The same reprimand spoken by a housekeeper or babysitter does not have the same impact. Moreover, it is our own personal values and traditions that we want to pass on to our children, not those of babysitters and housekeepers.

Even if we could find the perfect Mary Poppins, we would still be sending our children mixed messages by turning over the precious years of their childhood to someone outside the family circle. And as most people discover, Mary Poppinses are few and far between. I remember the anguish of a medical student who went to a counselor about whether she should complete medical school or drop out to raise a family. The counselor suggested that she could do both with a little outside help. The student explained that she had vowed never to entrust her children to a housekeeper. The counselor asked why, and the young woman explained that when she was a young child, her wealthy parents would vacation in Europe each summer and leave her with a nanny. One spring when the girl was eleven the housekeeper suddenly quit. The parents were upset that their vacation was jeopardized, but a few days before their intended departure they found a replacement. When the daughter noticed her mother wrapping up all the family silverware and jewels, she asked her why, since it had never been done before. Her mother explained that she could not trust the new maid with the family valuables. That insensitive remark stabbed the little girl in the heart. Was she not a "family valuable" of more worth than knives and forks?! She never forgot the incident and as she grew up she promised herself that she would bring up her own children.

Sometimes we rationalize leaving children alone or with babysitters by asserting that they must learn to be independent. We don't want to be overprotective. "Be a man!" we tell our sons. "Be independent and learn to handle things alone." "It's time to be on your own and start breaking away." "It's an impersonal world out there and you have to learn to deal with it." How different these exhortations sound from the words, "Be a mensch!" No, the true mark of menschlichkeit is not independence but admitting our need for other people.

We sell our children a false bill of goods when we force them to be on their own too soon as if independence and autonomy are the highest human values. Our obsession with individualism, independence, and the self, rather than interdependence, relationship, and responsibility, masks our need for other people. Our excessive preoccupation with ourselves is reflected in the very words that dominate our language: self-realization, self-actualization, self-fulfillment, self-discovery. Why do we hear the statement "I don't need any help" as a mark of maturity rather than as a pathetic cry of aloneness or a statement of arrested development? A Manhattan woman describes the latch-key adults she sees every day in her neighborhood on the Upper East Side: "At six or seven o'clock in my neighborhood near the United Nations I see all these single men and women, all nattily clad, loading up on serve-yourself salads in the local produce markets. Then they take their plastic cartons of salad and go across the street to pick up their nightly movie from the video rental. Finally, armed for the night, they go home, sit down, eat their salads, and turn on the VCR."

You cannot be a mensch in isolation. A life of loneliness, even though it be quiet and tranquil, is a diminished life. A Yiddish folksaying expresses the idea in three short words: One is none. Being single or living isolated from other people may be a temporary necessity and we can sometimes admire people who because of fate or circumstances beyond their control have made the best of a lonely situation without surrendering to despair; but this self-reliance is a shabby model to hold forth for our ~dren. Walden Pond was not a permanent address even ~or Thoreau, who returned to Concord claiming he had other lives to live. The purpose of life goes beyond being able to live contentedly with oneself. We must learn to live with other people. Interdependence is the touchstone of maturity. Men and women need one another. Our children need us, even as we need them.

Within the emotional warmth and richness of the family we discover the possibility for intimate and satisfying relationships with other human beings. The hundreds of small transactions of everyday life between parent and child convince our children that someone is crazy about them, loves them, is passionately concerned about the kind of people they will become. The family, where we learn to love, trust, and be responsible to others, is the basic web of existence, not the individual. Life begins in the womb of someone who loves you, and if you're lucky, death finds you surrounded by others who have come to know and love you too.

No one would deny that a measure of independence is a worthy ideal. Children cannot be dependent upon us forever, nor should we want them to be. They have their own lives to live. But independence is the beginning of the journey, not the end. The famous rabbinic sage Hillel proclaimed in the first century, "If I am not for myself, who is for me? And if I am *only* for myself what am I?"

A story by Y. L. Peretz, "Beside the Dying," extends Hillel's insight a bit further. A man lying on his deathbed is visited by an angel sent to whisk him off to heaven as soon as his last breath expires. Sensing the angel's presence, the fever-stricken man asks, "And what is life like up there in heaven, in paradise? What shall I be doing there?" The angel answers, "You won't have to do anything. There is eternal rest there, everlasting joy, and enduring happiness." Confused, the man turns toward the angel. "Is anyone there whom I can help? Can I raise up the dejected, heal the sick, feed the hungry, or give water to parched lips?" "No," the angel replies, "no one will need your help there." Distraught, the man decides, "Where there is no one who needs my soul, my heart, my tear of pity, my word of comfort, or my hand to lift them up, there is nothing for me to do." The man refuses to go with the angel and asks, "Could I be reassigned?"

The richest rewards in this life (and perhaps the world to come) arise from lives lived with other people and the time we take to help them when they are in need. Raising children to be menschen is a time-consuming task for fathers and mothers—not a job assignment for others. When we raise our children to be menschen, we give them a worthy goal in this life and perhaps a taste of heaven.

3. Bringing Up Superbaby

I think parents should forget the genius bit—what you want is a human being, a mensch, not a genius.

—JEROME BRUNER

When my youngest daughter Ariella was ten months old, my wife and I received an invitation to an open house for a program which promised to give her a head start in learning. Like most parents we responded favorably to terms like "head start" and "learning." The literature promised that during the forty-five-minute weekly classes, our daughter would play on equipment specially designed to stimulate her "balance, touch, and muscle-joint systems" which we were told were critical for future learning. The promotional brochure informed us that because half of all learning occurs in the first four years of a child's life, it was important that our daughter's play have a purpose. Apparently there wasn't a minute to lose.

Curious about the program and concerned for Ariella's future as well as her muscle-joint systems, we decided to attend the orientation. On a cold, overcast Friday morning

I took Ariella to a local community center where we entered a large room filled with equipment. I was given a warm smile and a name tag with which to identify my daughter. The room was filled with hoops, slides, tires, rockers, mirrors, and balls. It was a wonderful playground, and we were eager to dive in and start playing. The literature, however, had warned us that play had to be "purposeful," and soon we were sitting quietly in a circle with twenty-five babies ranging from three months to one year, attentively listening to the program director promise that the class would give us "quality time" with our children. The session began. Our first "purposeful" activity was the manipulation of the babies' arms and legs to improve muscle tone. My daughter had always shown a keen instinct in manipulating her own limbs and decided that the best way to do it in this circle was to crawl out of it. Other babies had the same idea.

That exercise over, the tots were put into a large, colorful inverted parachute which was spun by the parents as we walked in a circle. This activity had an even lower survival rate, and most of us had to remove our crying infants before it officially ended. The orientation concluded with the group leader singing a song as she walked around the circle with a puppet bobbing up and down on a stick. Predictably Ariella reached out to grab the puppet, not realizing that this was a "stretch only" activity and not a "touch" one. Unable to play with the puppet, she left the orientation grumpy and ill-tempered. "Purposeful playing" for "future growth and learning" were concepts to which she did not respond.

As we left the building I stopped to read a poster on the

bulletin board which explained the philosophy of the session we had just attended. It read:

> The program is based on a concept of integrative play. It takes the principles of sensory integration theory, theories of neurological organization and psycho-motor therapy, basic knowledge of motor development, and physical fitness and combines them in a creative mix of learning and fun. . . . The equipment was selected by professional educators for stimulating sensory-motor and learning skills. It is selected to stimulate the Vestibular (balancing), Proprioceptive (muscle-joint feedback), and Tactile (touch) systems with strong input to the visual and auditory systems.

I struggled to decipher the jargon and decided it wasn't worth it. Why did skills which children had always learned in the daily rounds of family life now have to be taught by professionals and—what's more—be learned before the age of one!? Worse, why did it require specialized language to describe them? I got the distinct feeling it was primarily to intimidate parents into believing that they were inadequate. I didn't stick around to find out. If Ariella had failed her orientation, so what? We left quickly and went home to the cluttered kitchen where we had great fun playing on the floor with the pots and pans.

It may be unfair to judge a program only by its orientation and promotional literature, but this particular program reflects an approach to childhood and childrearing which is increasingly widespread. In Philadelphia a widely touted program trains parents to enhance the intellectual development of their children and upon completion certifies parents are "professional" mothers and fathers. The first grade curriculum in this licensed school includes advanced Eng-

lish language, Greek and Latin word roots, analytical ge-
ometry, computer science, Japanese language and culture,
violin ensemble, music theory, ballet, drawing and mara-
thon running. The program directors brag about one of
their first graders who "reads Dickens' classics, does research with an encyclopedia, reads and discusses with
Mom current events in the daily newspaper. Mom began
teaching her daughter at the age of eighteen months. Her
daughter was reading library books at three years, novels
and the encyclopedia at four years." This student and
others are hailed as evidence that very young children can
perform amazing feats of intelligence. The leaders of the
Philadelphia program assert that even infants as young as
eight months can learn about "birds, their names, identifi-
cation, scientific classification, and habitats—about
flowers, trees, insects, reptiles, sea shells, mammals, fish,
presidents, kings, flags, jewels, nations, and states." I
know there's a lot more to learn today than a couple generations ago, but can't we save sea shells till later?

A New York City brochure urged parents to send their
one-year-olds to a readiness program to prepare them for
the "sharp competition" at selective nursery schools. In a
twenty-session cram course the program promoters promised to teach the preschoolers how to surmount the hurdle
of nursery school interviews. Lest anyone be ignorant of
the facts, the letter warned that the more selective nursery
schools accept only twenty to thirty students from eight
hundred applicants. I wonder why it didn't occur to them
to list the program's alumni, touting their later academic or
professional accomplishments!

Recently some advocates of early learning were inter-
viewed on public television. One mother in front of an

easel holding a graph with x and y coordinates explained that she spent eight hours each day teaching her four-year-old. Another mother and father sat at their kitchen table with their newborn baby and flipped flashcards in front of her which contained pictures of insects, reciting the name of each in Latin. A third mother described how she began teaching her child during the fifth month of pregnancy and proudly boasted that each of her children could speak full sentences by the age of three months. Perhaps public television should pilot a program called "Romper Womb" for those parents who want to give their children an exceptionally early start!

The promise behind all these programs and books for early learning is that they will lead to a prestigious college, the fast track, and success in life. I'm sure many graduates do well by these standards, but I wonder how many would have been just as successful—and perhaps happier—without this early rush to win the academic sweepstakes. I'm afraid the fast track is often just that: a fast track leading to stress, emotional turmoil, self-doubts, and unmanageable pressure. How early do we want to place our children on that kind of track?

I sit as a member on an elementary school board that recently discussed whether to continue to administer standardized tests to first graders. The question arose because some students were showing physical signs of stress in anticipation of the exams. A Massachusetts school system recently began a course on stress management for its fifth-graders. School administrators anticipated an enrollment of eight students. Thirty applied. The school psychologist explained, "Just the everyday pressures in school are great, such as peer pressure to do well. It's amazing what full lives youngsters have. They have no free time. It's just go, go, go, and often they just can't sleep."

It isn't just children but entire families that get "over-programmed"—parents chauffeuring their young ones from soccer league to tennis lessons to dancing class. One mother told me how she panicked one summer when her children planned to spend the entire summer at home: no school, no camp, no leagues or lessons. "I dreaded the thought. What would I do with them each day?" And what did they do? "We just spent time with each other," she recalls. "It was the most relaxed two months we ever had!" It can be done.

When we suggest to our children that the only important goals in life are grades, a good college, and success, the pressure to compete and win may become the only focus of their lives. They may feel that we value them for their grades and academic success rather than for being good people. I know of parents who give their kids a cash bonus for every A they get on report cards. One of my colleagues simply put his arm over his teenage son's shoulder one evening while he was doing homework. The boy threw off his dad's hand with the rebuke, "Come on, Dad, you only put your arm around me when I'm working, never when we are just talking or watching TV." Even when we may not intend it, we give our children the message that we love them for what they achieve, not for who they are. We ignore them when they are thoughtful, generous, or kind and only praise them when they produce.

Some children go to extremes to produce in order to measure up. Cheating has become widespread in our schools because "making it" has crowded out other values. One of my own students cynically observed, "There is no payoff for not cheating." Our children know that grades and activities will be important for college. They are not so sure integrity will make a difference. Another pragmatic student told me that religious studies are irrelevant for admission to college. How sad if he is right.

Such children are already victims of a "me-ism" that demands more satisfaction from material success than it can possibly offer. Many are headed for sad disillusionment later in life. Occasionally I run across a young boy or girl who can see through the shallowness of such materialism. Recently a boy in my class wisely objected to the success ethic that drives so many of his peers, and my own generation, to make money and be number one in everything. "Why can't you just be the little guy who's happy," he asked, "instead of the big star that's got all sorts of problems?"

In his autobiography the statesman and philanthropist Bernard Baruch describes how he made his first million dollars at the age of twenty and then expected his father to jump for joy when he announced that he had become a millionaire. Instead his father calmly responded, "That's wonderful, Bernard, but tell me what will you do with this million dollars." Baruch was crushed, but later realized his father had given him a beautiful touchstone for true success. Throughout his life, as he continued to make millions, he always asked himself, "Bernard Baruch, what will you do with them?"

There is nothing wrong with "making it." A mensch does not have to espouse poverty or eschew success, but for a true mensch "making it" is not an end in itself. A parent in my community lamented: "My children and those of my friends are driven to make a lot of money. Don't get me wrong. I grew up in poverty and didn't want to spend the rest of my life in a hot, crowded tenement. I wanted to have money to make life a little better for my parents and to give my kids the education, the open space, and the time for themselves I never had. I try to give to the good causes which helped me. My kids, however, only want money to prove how successful they are."

Every child cannot be a winner. For every winner there are many losers. For every child who receives a first, second, or third prize, there are children who receive no prizes. Not everyone gains entrance into a selective nursery school, comes out in the top reading or math group, ranks number one in high school, gets into a "hot college," and rises to the top of his or her profession. If our children think that these are the only sources of self-worth, those who cannot be winners will not only see themselves as losers, they will view themselves as failures. The next step for them may be to drop out by way of drinking, drugs, or chronic depression. The doubling rate of teenage suicide, the sharp increase in premature sexual relations often leading to teenage pregnancies, the reliance on drugs, and routine drunkenness are not inevitable stages of growing up. They reflect a critical breakdown in a coherent set of values and standards which give order, meaning, and dignity to life.

The twelve-year-old who came home in tears because she did not get an academic award in school and asked, "Mommy, why don't they hand out prizes for just being nice?" had discovered a bitter truth about the modern world. There are no built-in rewards for decency. All the more reason it is incumbent upon us to see that our children know our love is not conditional upon their class rank, report cards, or victories in intramural sports. Those things can make us proud, but they do not make us love them. We love them simply because they are ours.

Why are we so obsessed with high achievement? Studies and biographies abound that dissect the early lives of the Mozarts, Einsteins, and Freuds of the world. In a recent study the lives of 120 superachievers, which included research mathematicians, Olympic swimmers, concert pianists, tennis players, sculptors, and neurologists, were assiduously analyzed along with interviews of their teachers and parents to determine what made them tick. Why are we not equally fascinated by people whose lives are outstanding examples of menschlichkeit? Why won't someone research the unusual neighbor who cooks meals for a family whose mother is sick, an individual who takes off time from work day after day to visit a friend in the hospital, a person who always has time to listen sympathetically to the problems of a colleague? Do we not care about the roots and origins of outstanding kindness, compassion, and concern for other people? Were the 120 superachievers also decent and responsible individuals?

The pressure to be a superparent is as intense as the pressure to be a superchild. Each of us, in our own subtle ways, flashes the reading cards in front of our three-month-old just to keep the doors open. We live in a society that markets high achievement and we want the best for our children. We seek reassurance that two careers, single parenthood, or a housekeeper have not harmed our children. In our rush to be perfect parents to perfect children, we have stopped trusting our common sense and parental instincts. We want to buy every toy for fear we will deprive our children of important learning experiences. Whereas

ke of a deprived child as one who lacked the
ssities of life, today a deprived background is a
is not festooned with mirrors, mobiles, music
box and bells.

It is easy to lose confidence in our natural ability to raise
children. The true techniques for raising children are simple: Be with them, play with them, talk to them. You are
not squandering their time no matter what the latest child
development books say about "purposeful play" and "cog-
nitive learning skills." In spite of our worries to the contrary, children are still being born with the innate ability to
learn spontaneously, and neither they nor their parents need
the sixteen-page instructional manual that came with a rat-
tle I recently ordered for Eytan, our baby boy!

Thousands of books have been published in recent years
which explain every detail of the apparently overwhelming
task of rearing alert and intelligent children. Books with
titles like *How to Teach Your Baby to Read*, *How to Teach
Your Baby Math*, *How to Multiply Your Baby's Intelligence*, *Blueprint for a Brighter I.Q.*, *How to Raise Your
Child's I.Q.*, and *How to Raise Your Child to Be a Winner*
contain chapters which suggest that we can make geniuses
out of every child: "The Plasticity of a Young Child's
Brain," "Parents as a Child's Most Crucial Teacher,"
"Guidelines for Enriching a Child's Learning Environ-
ment," and "Raising a Superstar." There are books on the
first twelve months of development, the second twelve
months, and on all the days in between and the years there-
after.

As parents we hesitate to make a move without the appropriate book or manual. Sam Levenson tells a wonderful
story about the birth of his first child. The first night home

the baby would not stop crying. His wife frantically flipped through the pages of Dr. Spock to find our why babies cry and what to do about it. Now, since Spock's book is rather long, the baby cried a long time. Grandma was in the house, but since she had not read the books on childrearing, she was not consulted. The baby continued to cry. Finally, Grandma could be silent no longer. "Put down the book," she told her children, "and pick up the baby."

Some books do help us deal with specific problems and are a valuable source of reassurance and comfort in a moment of worry or need. We are better advised and more educated than any other generation of parents. Yet this deluge of literature and advice can also leave us feeling overwhelmed and inadequate. Where is the joy of bringing a child into the world if we are always afraid of making a mistake? If raising children becomes a research project, then we had better take the right courses and read the latest books because we will question our competence at every turn. Are we loving too much or too little? Are we underprotecting or overprotecting? Undernourishing or overnourishing? Pushing too hard or not enough? Every word can be taken the wrong way. A wrong move today may return to haunt our children thirty years from now on a therapist's couch!

Parenting is too important to hand it over to the experts. It is a serious and painstaking responsibility that should spur us to evaluate our personal commitments and priorities. What values do we want to pass on to the next generation? What is the right way to live? What kind of world do we want our children to live in? So many of the experts never ask these questions. They assume that knowing what to do with our children is a matter of appropriate technique

an appropriate values; of structuring, program-
d age-grading a child's day rather than shaping our
own ves to be worthy models. We are not simply placement agencies locating the right programs and activities for
our children. Nor need we bring the same professionalism,
efficiency, and push for achievement to childrearing that
we bring to our careers. We have forgotten that childrearing is really child-loving, not an exercise in time management or performance evaluation. We do not need an army
of management consultants to advise us. We may be one-
minute managers at the office, but let's not be one-minute
parents at home.

So-called professional childrearing is based on a narrow
conception of what it means to be a child, as well as an
adult. It is based on a cult of achievement which states that
intellectual advancement is the highest good and that the
right information, stimulation, and age-appropriate developmental tasks will turn children into intelligent adults. A
young child is no longer simply a child; he or she is a
preschooler, poised at the starting gate in the race of life.

Children are not only receptacles for knowledge, they
are human beings who have likes and dislikes, who laugh
and lose their temper, succeed, stumble, and get back up
again. Sometimes they need a pat on the back, reassurance,
or a hug; sometimes to be reminded that they are not the
center of the world. Through it all they need the constant
love of parents who think their kids are tops.

Intelligence is an important trait in a mensch; knowing
the responsible, fair, and decent thing to do in any situation
requires a finely honed sense of right and wrong which can
emerge from study. Yet I.Q. alone is not a measure of
character or wisdom. Honors classes, making the dean's

list, taking advanced placement classes, and doing well on the College Boards did not make me a better person or attest to my character. My fellow college students were highly intelligent, but there was nothing particularly unusual about their moral character. They were a normal mixture of ethical and unethical individuals akin to what you would find in any group of eighteen- to twenty-two-year-olds.

Education will not ensure menschlichkeit, and recent history shows this beyond a doubt. When the Nazis seized power they found plenty of ideological support and sympathy within German universities. If morality were a result of education we would expect to find the German universities at the forefront of the opposition to Nazism. They were not. There is simply no causal link between modern secular education and being a mensch. Education can produce academic and professional skills but may not develop menschlichkeit.

Menschlichkeit develops earlier in life than we sometimes think. When Beth, the daughter of two of our friends, began kindergarten, she came home each day and claimed she never had time for recess. Her parents quizzed her on what she did all day but could not understand why she was never able to go outside and play. Finally they spoke with the teacher and learned that each day Beth helped a girl with crutches down the steps. The other children would brush the handicapped student aside in their hurry to go out and play, but Beth stayed behind to help at the expense of her own free time. She never mentioned it to her parents because it never occurred to her that this was anything but an ordinary thing to do. The parents told me that their daughter always felt a special sensitivity to others, and it's no mystery to figure out where she picked this up. Beth's parents always treat one another with kindness and consideration, and compassion is simply one of the hallmarks of family life for them.

It is easy to spot the beginnings of kindness and cruelty in young children. A mother told me that her daughter Amy was upset each day when she returned home. After a week in first grade the girl suddenly blurted out the reason. Some of the girls in her class had formed a clique with a secret password. The girls not only excluded Amy from the club but teased her, broke her pencils, emptied glue on her desk, and told her she was fat and ugly.

I do not know what this mother told Amy, but I do remember our own discomfort when we learned that Naamit, our middle daughter, was part of a first-grade clique with passwords, secret rituals, and exclusionary membership policies to remind some of the six-year-olds that they were outside the inner circle. We were happy that Naamit had grown comfortable with a group of close friends, but we were upset that other children were left out. As we spoke to her, we realized she had no idea that anyone was getting hurt. We were relieved a few weeks later when she and her best friend announced they had formed a new club with a special membership rule: "Everyone can join!"

The capacity for kindness begins as early as the capacity for selfishness. Some two-year-olds naturally offer a parent some of their food; others eat it all themselves. Some four-year-olds instinctively embrace a younger sister or brother who is crying; others ignore the tears. Some five-year-olds take a walk in the field and pick flowers to bring to their mothers; others simply trample the grass. A recent study has shown that the beginnings of altruism can be seen in children as early as the age of two. How then can we be so concerned that they count by the age of three, read by four, and walk with their hands across the overhead parallel bars by five, and not be concerned that they act with kindness to others?

Schools are places where children can learn to get along with other children, and classroom lessons can sensitize them to ethical concerns and help them grow toward menschlichkeit. Yet the most powerful lessons about ethics and morality do not come from school discussions or classes in character building. They come from family life where people treat one another with respect, consideration, and love.

Take the time to point out to your children the consequences of their actions. Let them know when others get hurt through their insensitivity or when a kind deed makes someone else feel good. Children are entitled to their privacy, but there is nothing wrong when a parent tells a teenager that he used his girlfriend in a relationship and then dropped her when he no longer needed her. If our children do not hear from us about the effects of what they do, no one else is likely to have enough time or concern to tell them.

A child's struggling efforts to be considerate should never be ignored or belittled. One of my friends has never forgotten a moment in her own childhood when she picked a bouquet of dandelions from the front lawn to present to her mother while she was waiting for everyone to climb into the family car. The girl proudly handed the bouquet to her mother who harshly told her to "get rid of those weeds!" Even today the woman has never forgotten that moment when an expression of love for her mother was so coldly rejected.

Our own daughter Ilana was the first in her second grade class to wear an orthodontic brace. Afraid the other students would tease her, she got up in front of the class the day before she first wore the brace to explain why she had to wear it. The teacher, sensing Ilana's fear, spent the next few days discussing with the class the reasons people wear corrective devices such as glasses, casts, and crutches. The discussions helped everyone understand the situation, including Ilana.

We do not always know what our children are thinking and even the most sensitive parents will inadvertently hurt a child's feelings. Yet we can all be more alert to reinforce acts of kindness whenever they occur. It may be an older sibling volunteering to help a younger one with homework; a child going out of his way to help around the house; a little one's thank-you note written for a gift. These are the lessons we should be quick to teach and reinforce. If we focus exclusively on teaching our children to read, write, spell, and count in their first years of life, we turn our homes into extensions of school and turn bringing up a child into an exercise in curriculum development. We should be parents first and teachers of academic skills second.

There are times in our children's lives when we will have to be academic coaches, but let's hope they look to us as much for the right way to live as for the right answers to class exercises. Our homes do not have to be seats of early learning but they should be cradles of warmth, love, caring, sharing, tears, and laughter. A home filled with the vibrant fullness of life is more important than a home filled

with the right toys and the proper childrearing tech
Gently nurture your children in the techniques of living and
acting like menschen. When a baby holds a blanket over
his eyes and a mother spontaneously responds with "pee-
kaboo!" the boy's concept of self-worth begins to develop.
When a daughter pulls off her father's hat and puts it on her
own head and dad laughs heartily as he takes it back, she
begins to understand that she can make someone else
happy. When a baby waves good-by and blows a kiss for
the first time, wave back and return the kiss. In fact, how
can you not? The expressions of menschlichkeit are wonderfully contagious; and in these natural responses of parent and child, a mensch is born.

Learning, reading books, discussing school work can all
be part of the normal love and fabric of family life. But
take your cues from your children, rather than flashing cue
cards at them. We want children who will love learning and
value intelligence, but we do not teach these things by designing a course of study. We teach them by listening, responding, discussing, and doing things together.

We must be careful not to give our children the wrong
message: that our love is conditional upon their accomplishments. We must love them whether or not they make
good grades, go out for extracurricular activities, make the
best colleges, take piano and skating lessons. When a
grown daughter someday tells us about the man she hopes
to marry, will we first ask "What does he do?" instead of
"Is he a decent person?"

If our children feel that they are loved for what they do
rather than for who they are, they will find it hard to love
themselves; and a person who does not love him or herself
will have a hard time loving others. Trite jokes abound

brags about her son, the doctor. No
er son, the mensch. Too often I hear
ll, at least so-and-so is a good person."

g a good person become the _least_ thing we
ut another? And are we raising children who
will eday find that this is the _least_ thing they can say
about themselves?

The Talmud, a code of Jewish law composed in the early part of the first century, states that when a child is born it is approached by an angel who requires that the child take a simple oath: "Be righteous, and never be wicked." (Niddah 3ob.) A child is not asked to be precocious, smart, clever, or class valedictorian. A child is asked to become a mensch—caring, fair, decent. If by chance the child goes on to become the best at something, fine. A genuine mensch can handle success—and failure, too.

In some ways the promotional brochures about getting a head start in life are right, but their focus is wrong. Our children need a "heart start" in the virtues of menschlich-keit. The schools can help our children's minds grow smarter. It is up to us to ensure that their hearts grow warmer.

4. Activist Parenting

*Train up a child in the way he should go, and
even when he is old, he will not depart from it.*
—PROVERBS 22:6

"All happy families resemble one another, but each unhappy family is unhappy in its own way." So observed
Tolstoy in the opening lines of *Anna Karenina*. And there
in a nutshell is one of the major reasons we find it hard to
know how to raise a mensch: No one wants to write about
the sameness of happy families. There is more drama in
conflict and tragedy than there is in harmony and well-
being, and so menschlichkeit is not the subject of best-sell-
ing novels, popular movies, or television shows that
substitute wise-cracking children and fumbling, befuddled
parents for genuine characters we really could emulate.
Even neighborhood gossip is about the fights and arguments of local families rather than the less dramatic acts of
kindness and consideration. It would be easier for us to
know how to raise a mensch if we had believable models
steeped in menschlichkeit.

Unhappy families may be the inspiration for better, more absorbing literature, but they are not the source of better children. One literary portrayal of menschlichkeit has remained with me over the years because of its beauty and simplicity. The short story "The Kerchief" by Nobel Prize winner Shmuel Yosef Agnon is based on a young man's reminiscence of his childhood in Eastern Europe around the end of the nineteenth century.

Each year the narrator's father would leave home for a week to sell his wares in the marketplace of Lashkowitz. The week his father was gone was like a week of mourning. Smiles and laughter vanished from the house, the mother stood her vigil before the window, her eyes moist with tears, she and the children waiting eagerly the day of father's return. He would enter the house, sweep up his wife and each of the children in his arms, and give them a gift and a kiss.

One year he brought an exceptionally beautiful silk kerchief with embroidered flowers as a token of his love for his wife. Every Friday afternoon the boy's mother would set the table with a white cloth and two braided loaves of bread. As the last rays of sunlight faded in the west, she would cover her hair with the kerchief and light the Sabbath candles.

On the day the boy turned thirteen and went to synagogue to be called before the congregation, his mother tied her kerchief around his neck as a token of her love for him. On the way home the boy passed a beggar in the street, his hands swollen and his feet covered with sores. Hesitantly, the boy handed him his mother's kerchief to bind up his wounds, and then he returned home anxious that he had parted with one of his mother's dearest posessions. The love in his mother's eyes reassured him that ... his kind act toward the beggar as his initiatio... hood. The parents' love for each other had b... wellspring of compassion now flowing through the..., reaching out toward others in need.

Years later the boy, now a man himself, recalls the father's homecomings of so long ago: "I look about me now to try to find something to which to compare my father when he stood together with his tender children, yet I can find nothing pleasant enough. But I hope that the love haloing my father of blessed memory may wrap us round whenever we come to embrace our little children, and that joy which possessed us then will be possessed by our children all their lives."

This beautiful short story is suffused with a family's love and compassion, seen most strikingly in the father and mother who are exemplary models of kindness for their children. Being models for our children and transmitting a moral tradition are the most important duties in raising them to be menschen. No lengthy list of childrearing techniques will guarantee a mensch better than our own example. By creating a climate of warmth, affection, and expectation we make it easier for our children to incorporate into their own lives the best that is within us.

It is in the nature of children to imitate. But we must actively make the effort to provide them with something worthy of imitation. It is not possible to be effective parents if we are frequently gone or uninvolved in our children's daily lives, or if we do not in some way make up for the times when obligations do prevent us from being with them. There are many influences on children: television, movies, books, magazines, their schools, the friends they

...ng around with. All have the power to shape their values by reinforcing or undermining the standards we set for them.

Being a shining model of menschlichkeit is not always easy. We may have never developed the knack of responding with patience and kindness because our own parents seldom did; much of our present style of parenting is based on them. Good intentions and the aggravating pressures of daily life may work against each other, and if we are honest with ourselves we would have to admit that many times we don't know what the menschlich thing to do really is. Good intentions and abundant love are crucial, but they do not ensure that we will always be good models for our children.

Being modern men and women we cannot escape the cult of the expert. We would like someone to hand us a thoroughly researched, tried, and tested blueprint for raising our children to be menschen. We would like to have instruction sheets on when to show anger and when to control it, when to express love and when to hide it, when to be strict and when lenient, when to make decisions for our children and when to let them choose for themselves. Yet there can be no precise formulas. Our children are too unique. Family life is too fluid. Menschlichkeit ultimately emerges from the love and respect we have for our children and they for us.

I know of no way to train an activist parent; nor have I ever seen a thirty-day program for making a mensch. The suggestions which follow are not a manual of menschlichkeit. Rather they are attitudes and habits of mind to meet the daily realities of life with our children. I offer them as general illustrations of ways we can reinforce menschlichkeit in specific situations, ways to reveal the best in our-selves in front of our children so that they grow up with their own memories of how our love "haloed" them.

Listening

Children want to be heard and understood. They need us to listen and understand. At some point every child is the victim of bullying, teasing, or ostracism and comes home in tears. At times every child feels ignored, misunderstood, or inadequate. The matter may seem trivial to us, we know it will pass; but to the child, the whole world has just fallen apart. Sometimes we will be able to help, sometimes we may not. We cannot fight every battle for our children, yet it makes all the difference in the world to them if they know we are behind them supporting them all the way.

Our children's feelings are as real as our own. It doesn't help to belittle their feelings by responding with the old cliches: "You'll get over it," "It will pass," "You're too old to worry about that," or the real clinker: "When I was your age, things were much worse." Our children's fear or worry will not vanish because we deny it. Denying it sim-ply makes the child feel all the more alone. Better openers are statements like: "Perhaps you are feeling . . . ," "It sounds to me as if . . . ," "If I understand you, you are saying. . . ." We are not amateur psychologists, but with the right words we let our children know that we under-stand them and take their feelings seriously. By helping them find words to express what's bothering them, we can help them begin to manage their emotions, clarify their thoughts, and talk openly about their problems instead of lashing out whenever they are frustrated. While simply reflecting a child's words back is not enough, it is a start; and it may be the start of an important conversation your child has long been wanting to have with you.

I remember the incident of Scott, a four-year-old who for some mysterious reason refused to sit next to his grandfather at the table. He would put up a fuss everytime the grandparents came to dinner. The boy's parents tried talking with him to discover what the problem was, but it didn't help. What made it more perplexing was that Scott had formerly enjoyed, even asked, to sit next to grandpa. The change occurred at the grandfather's eightieth birthday party. Months went by, and the young boy was adamant about not sitting next to grandpa. Then the grandmother made an off-hand remark that Scott seemed to be "afraid of his grandfather." When the boy heard that, he admitted that he was afraid. On questioning by his parents, Scott revealed that he had heard his father remark that people seldom lived beyond age eighty, and the young boy was scared that his now eighty-year-old grandfather would expire right next to him at dinner. Because the grandmother had voiced Scott's fear, the boy was able to bring it up and talk about it. Such is often the case, and once the words are out in the open, parents are then able to reassure children that many of their fears are groundless.

Praise

Every child needs to be praised now and then. But praise is like the sun. If it is too direct or strong, in a short time it will burn. We turn red with embarrassment. Exaggerated praise, even when given with the best intentions, can sound like pressure or a warning. "You are always such a good kid," "You never give us any problems," or "You don't have a mean bone in your body." We say it as praise. The child hears it as a warning to be good or a threat as to what might happen if he's not. None of our children is perfect and, what's more, each child knows it! Few children can live up to such accolades. Life on a pedestal is treacherous, and the wise child may simply climb down. We are usually better off praising what they do rather than what they are. Praise their good behavior rather than their character. The same is true of misbehavior: scold the mischief, not the mischief-maker. If we repeatedly say, "You're a bad kid" or "You will grow up to be a good-for-nothing," a child may feel honor bound to live up to it.

Once I called in the parents of Danny, a twelve-year-old student who was making no effort in his work and had become disruptive in class. They threw up their hands in despair and told me they had tried everything and come to the conclusion that their son was stupid. It was clear to me that Danny had gotten the message that it was safer not to do any work and to make a joke of everything than to try his best and come off looking stupid. Three years later there was a dramatic change. He became one of the most enthusiastic kids, volunteered for everything, and eventually became a class leader. Again I spoke to the parents and learned that Danny had discovered computers, and computers seemed to have discovered him. They were made for each other! Other kids came to him for advice and he had even earned some money designing programs. That was all it took for him to realize that to expend so much energy proving that he was stupid was—to put it mildly—stupid! He had too much talent for that! Every child has talent, something he or she is better at than most other kids. Allowing our children to pursue those interests from which they derive a sense of accomplishment does wonders for their self-confidence.

There's a wise old riddle about being able to distinguish the dancer from the dance. Can you? Can you distinguish your child's behavior from who that child really is? Praising our children, as well as reprimanding them, requires us to walk the fine edge of that riddle. Praise what they do well, and love them when they do not do well. They are still the same individuals. Children need to feel that whatever the rest of the world may think, mother and dad believe completely in their talent whether they are the best or far from the best. If dancing lessons begin to transform an awkward, gawky pre-teen into a graceful, poised young lady, we can make her feel that she has conquered the world. What the dancing lessons begin to accomplish, our praise will help complete. And so with anything. A child may build self-confidence by constructing a treehouse in the backyard or taking the family car apart (and hopefully putting it back together!); some children discover their unique talents on a soccer field or in a chemistry lab or an art studio. If we can help our kids feel good about what they do, they will begin to feel good about themselves, and they will find the security and confidence to feel good about others.

So often in families we take one another's feelings for granted. We need to remind one another from time to time that we appreciate others' efforts to make family life pleasant. It doesn't take much. All we need say is, "I really appreciate your help," "What you did for me ~~~ nice," "I know it wasn't easy," or "I'm very proud ~~~ you acted,"; and our children will realize that we do notice them, listen to them, and really hear what they are trying to say.

Our Saturday morning tradition is to let the children get up before us to scurry down to the kitchen to set the table for breakfast. They climb up on chairs to reach cabinets and counters, haul down the cereals, and get the juices out of the refrigerator. It isn't always easy for them to remember who likes what and to match up the plates and bowls and silverware. And of course it takes them thirty-five minutes to do what my wife and I could do in five. But the kids are always proud of their achievement and it makes their day when we compliment them and tell them how good the table looks. In their own way, they feel that they are important.

A child who feels loved and valued, heard and understood, and knows that he is taken seriously, is on the way to becoming a mensch who will love, value, and appreciate the worth of others.

Setting Limits

Warmth, love, and praise alone, however, do not make a mensch. The Beatles song, "All You Need Is Love," should never become a theme song for childrearing. Love and praise alone can breed an unbridled permissiveness and self-indulgence that we so often see in the typical "spoiled child." No, the "soft" techniques of childrearing must be balanced with the "firm" ones of setting limits and expecting our children to adhere to worthy standards of behavior.

One of the ways we show our love is by showing that we care enough to say no. We know we cannot let an infant touch a hot stove, a four-year-old play with knives, nor can we let an eleven-year-old play fireman on the roof. As children grow older there are many things they learn for themselves, but there will always be times when they need a restraining hand. A few decades ago the phrases *Es past nisht*—it's not right; *Me tor nisht*—one doesn't do such a thing; *Es iz nisht bekovodik*—it's not the proper thing to do—were common Yiddish expressions among Jewish families. Certain things were not right and a child knew what they were. Children knew when they were wrong. You were not rude to your parents; you did not show disrespect to your teacher; you did not betray your friend; you did not turn your back on someone who needed help. Of course, children sometimes rebelled against these standards, but at least there was a clear set of rules against which to rebel.

Saying no and setting limits must always be done with the understanding that no one is perfect, neither our kids, nor us. Unduly harsh and strict rules do not make a perfect household. We all know children who grew up in authoritarian families and have never stopped rebelling against restrictiveness wherever they find it. And they seem to be more prone than others to find it! The goal is not boarding-school discipline or unquestioning obedience. Perfectly behaved children may not mature into perfectly behaved adults. A passively acquiescent child may turn into an actively resentful adult. Being coerced to say the right words and follow all the rules teaches children rebellion, not manners.

Today so much rebellion is aimless and demoralizing precisely because children have no values to challenge. Teenage rebellion is a testing process in which young people try out various values in order to make them their own. But during those years of trial, error, and embarrassment, a child needs family standards to fall back on, reliable habits of thought and feeling that provide security and protection. At times a child will provocatively misbehave in a desperate search for boundaries, for some clear sign that his parents care enough to stop him. We must remember that in spite of tears and anger, a child knows, on some deeper level, that our refusal to tolerate unacceptable behavior is a sign of our love.

Friends of ours are health nuts. Their teenage daughter is considerably overweight because she goes on junk food binges whenever she is out with her friends. Her constant complaint is that there is "never anything good to eat at home." She may have a point since her parents keep little else around than grains, sprouts, and fibers! After repeated arguments over her outside eating habits, our friends realized it wasn't right for them to foist their own eating standards on their daughter at her age. So they struck a deal. She promised to cut down on the junk food in exchange for being allowed to plan the family menu five nights a week. The girl has lost weight and she now feels loved and appreciated. The new arrangement gives her the measure of freedom and independence that she can handle.

It is our responsibility to set standards about how our children behave, how late they stay out, and whom they bring home. An unsupervised party in a midwestern community recently ended in needless tragedy. A group of teenagers had gathered to drink in the home of a boy whose parents were out of town. When the party broke up at 2:00 A.M., some of them continued their revelry out on the street. A young man passed on a bicycle and some of the kids shouted a threat at him. The cyclist pulled a gun and waved it to ward off the boys. Challenged and too drunk to let it pass, they hopped in a car and drove after the man, caught up with him, and knocked him off his bike. He pulled out his gun again and killed one of the boys.

At least some lessons were learned from this tragedy. In hundreds of communities parents have banded together to sign pledges not to allow drugs or liquor at their children's parties and to be home to supervise. It takes only a few parents who care enough and who do not want their own standards to be held hostage by other adults too busy or too wrapped up in themselves to set limits for their children.

How do we know where to draw the line? How many late evenings are too many? How late is too late? There are no precise answers to these questions. Certainly we cannot expect one solution to last from the cradle to college nor the same approach to work with each child. Such rigidity is unrealistic. The best guideline is simply to be sensitive to the uniqueness and individuality of each child, so that we know where they stand and they know where we stand.

We all learn that life is with other people, and living with them requires limits on our behavior. In the firm, loving structures of family life, a child learns that it's safe to deny oneself certain gratifications for the sake of others. Life does not come to an end when we discipline ourselves; in fact, it grows richer.

Mutual Respect

Mutual respect is an everyday part of raising children. Just as we care about our children's feelings, they also must learn to care about us. Children have their own legitimate feelings and opinions about things, but so do we. How often have we heard a child casually call a parent "stupid," "moron," or something even worse and then watch the parent ignore it? No anger, no demand for an apology, no punishment—just an embarrassed shrug of the shoulders.

The language we use in everyday life can either reflect that respect or its absence. We never know one another too well to omit "thank you" and "please." A mother recently wrote to an advice column in a newspaper complaining that she had not heard a thank you from her children in ten years! There is no excuse for eliminating the visible and tangible expressions of our respect for one another even on the assumption that we take our love for each other for granted. Menschlichkeit is much more than manners, but manners are part of the rich soil in which it grows. Manners do not necessarily indicate distance and coldness; they are more likely to be a sign of people trying to live harmoniously with each other. Allowing children to spew forth whatever is on their minds in the name of openness only creates an illusion of family closeness. A family that truly respects one another can be formal or informal as the occasion demands. They know they are close and that the closeness they value emerges from a loving commitment never to attack, humiliate, or disrespect each other.

In a moment of anger a child can find the sharpest words that, like arrows, cut and hurt deeply. Children know our vulnerable spots. "You are the worst parent!" "I hate you!" "I don't care what you say!" "What do you know anyhow?" "You've ruined my life!" When a child blows his top, it doesn't mean we have failed as parents or that we have raised callous children. All families have bad moments. Family members filled with love can lose their tempers and the family doesn't disintegrate. We want our children to find constructive ways to express their anger, and we should realize that one of the few places where they feel secure enough to vent that anger is at home. They may get reprimanded for a remark which goes too far, but they know they will not be expelled from the family. Tempers will cool, all will be forgiven, we will hug them once again.

Every family has fights, disagreements, stand-offs that arise not so much from disliking one another as from our difficulties in working out conflicts. There are four methods of dealing with conflict guaranteed to cut off any further discussion. Sarcasm: "Her royal highness can't go anyplace without her mirror!" Personal attacks: "You are a lousy good-for-nothing who would rather lie around the house all day than help!" Overpowering: "I have lived more years than you, young man, and I know what I'm talking about." Threats: "If you don't listen to me, you're grounded for the weekend!" All these responses undermine children's sense of self-worth, especially teenagers trying to figure out who they are, camouflaging their vulnerability beneath explosions of bravado. Sarcasm only begets more sarcasm. Personal attacks invite counteroffensives. Overpowering defines our children as losers. Threats escalate into all-out domestic warfare.

Ending an argument with very young children should be done quickly, and actions usually speak louder than words.

When my two-year-old walks off down the driveway after being told that it's time to go into the house because it's getting dark, there's nothing really to discuss. I scoop her into my arms with a hug, carry her into the house, and try to get her attention on something else.

With older children getting a problem out in the open and sometimes discussing it even to death is important. Fatiguing, but important. It shows that we value their opinions and feelings and want to hear them. "How do you feel about . . . ," "Tell me what's going on with. . . ." Invitations such as these will sometimes break through the Great Silence of Adolescence. On the other hand, "You will do this because I told you so" and "I'm your father and as long as you live under my roof you'll do as I say" are whammies that short-circuit any further dialogue. These comments clearly say to the child, "I don't want to hear what you have to say." They also make a child feel powerless and encourage him or her to wield power over others regardless of their feelings.

Sometimes with older children it may not be possible to work out a suitable compromise over some issue. When you feel you've discussed the problem beyond death and will never see eye to eye, it's best to end the matter clearly and decisively. A simple statement is better than long explanations or apologies. "I understand your reasons and have told you mine. I know what you want to do, but we have explained why it is not right and why we feel strongly about it. There are standards that we all follow in this family and we expect you to follow them too." Then hope for the best.

No child was ever destroyed by a moment of anger or impatience. Sometimes, in fact, an expression of genuine anger is a reminder that we care about them and love them. What destroys a child is an ongoing pattern of indifference, a deepening sense that his or her parents really don't care what happens. Too often children of cold, inexpressive parents will misbehave or rebel precisely to get their parents' attention. Punishment, even physical abuse, seems to some children better than being ignored.

We should give our children credit for being smarter and sometimes wiser than we imagine they are. They can handle our disappointment at something they have done; they can accept our anger when it is justified. As they grow older they will someday come to appreciate us for letting them know just where we stood on certain issues and just what the limits were.

Seeing Another's Viewpoint

"Walk a mile in my shoes" is good advice. Our children will learn to respect others if they are used to imagining themselves in another's place. If older children, for example, exclude a classmate from their social circle, we can discuss with our own children how they would feel if they were the outcasts. For younger children, a statement like "it hurts your baby brother when you give him a bear hug" helps the child understand the situation better than to simply say, "Don't give your baby brother a bear hug." The more accustomed our children are to understanding the consequences of their actions and viewing situations from a viewpoint other than their own, the more unlikely it is that they will think or act only for themselves.

It is our duty to create a framework in which a child can begin to understand other people's points of view, and yet we cannot undo the natural pattern of child development. Below a certain age children do not understand another person's feelings. The endless squabbles of younger children over toys and turf are usually not solved by saying, "Let me explain the situation from your younger sister's point of view." An angry and confused four-year-old really doesn't know—or care—how her younger sister feels. Yet when tempers subside and peace has been restored, we might take our children's puppets, toy people, or dolls and reenact the conflict. With a little humor—and a lot of playing it up, especially your kids' favorite expressions— you may even be able to get them to laugh at themselves. After reenacting the situation as it happened, then play it out in more considerate ways to show the children that there is always more than one way to solve a problem.

This may not work with older children who will accuse us of exaggerating or "getting it all wrong." But there are other creative ways for settling disputes. A mother told me she sometimes asks her eleven-year-old for permission to tape an early morning fight over choosing clothes or the daily combat over doing homework. It works wonderfully. Later her daughter admits that she "can't believe" how hysterical or panicky she had been. It can be a sobering experience. If you plan to try this method, be sure to ask permission to tape.

There are no simple rules or techniques that apply to every situation. Sometimes we send a child to his room until he calms down; but at other times this will only increase his sense of isolation and estrangement from the family. Even in a straightforward encounter where two children are fighting over a toy, we often have to play it by ear. The older children may be bullying a young one and we should intervene immediately and defend the younger child. On the other hand, if the older child takes a toy and the younger one grabs it back, we may want to stay out of it and hope the younger child learns to stand up for his rights. Sometimes a child will take a toy from someone in the belief that an absent friend to whom it belongs doesn't want the toy used. In this case we ought to praise the child for defending the rights of someone else. Peacekeeping missions onto our children's battlefields must always be launched with caution and respect for the uniqueness of each child and each situation.

Learning Responsibility

As children grow older they learn to become independent and self-reliant by making their own decisions based on their obligations and responsibilities to those around them. They learn responsibility by having responsibility. For very young children whose world is still bounded by the house and yard, responsibilities flow naturally from domestic realities: setting the table, cleaning up, bringing toys inside, helping younger brothers or sisters, straightening up their rooms. They may resist with whining complaints like "I'm too tired," "I did it yesterday," or "Why do you always ask me to do it?" An oaktag chart now hangs on the side of our refrigerator listing various chores such as setting the table, clearing it after meals, putting away toys, collecting garbage, sorting laundry. Down the side of the chart are the days of the week, and when Alisa and I need the children's help we can ward off complaints about not being fair by dividing up these jobs as equally as possible among all of us. Even when they don't really want to help, the kids are pretty good about pitching in when they realize that we're all in this together, even their mother and I.

Most parents find that children are more willing to help out if they can use their natural talents and know-how. Most children are thrilled when they realize they're big enough to provide "delivery service," such as bringing a cookie, a message, the mail, a newspaper to someone else. As a teenager I couldn't wait to run the family errands after receiving my driver's license. Alisa remembers how grown-up she felt when she accepted her first babysitting job. Match up chores with a child's growing sense of maturity, capitalizing on the skills and interests they are developing. When children know that we need their help because of a special talent or ability which they have or because it's clear we cannot do a task alone, they are more likely to help out.

On the other hand, if they perceive our demands as arbitrary or an attempt to foist upon them tasks we don't want to do ourselves, they may resist. We must remember there are some chores nobody wants to do, so we shouldn't be surprised if our kids try to squirm out of doing them. Family life is not a computer program that runs on its own; it needs continual input from everyone. As children learn that we assign tasks not for the sake of teaching them to do chores or out of some kind of parental perversity, but because we honestly need their help, they will come to see that their contributions are, in their own way, as important as our own.

mily we know keeps a large picture of a tree in their room. Whenever a member of the family demonstrates an unusual sense of responsibility, a leaf noting the event is added to the branches. The tree flourishes with good deeds and is always inspiring to look at. There are leaves indicating when the three-year-old cleaned up her toys without being told to do so, when the five-year-old wiped away the tears of his younger sister who had fallen and hurt herself, when the seven-year-old first made her bed, and when the eleven-year-old gave up a part of his allowance to send to the victims of an earthquake.

As children get older a part-time job or a volunteer activity will teach them to be accountable to others beyond the family circle. Making toys for hospitalized children, tutoring younger children, participating in a walk-a-thon to raise money, voluntering for a synagogue or church project, can instill a sense of responsibility. A march or a fundraising project could be an occasion for the entire family to work together and get to know each other in a different context from the usual humdrum of daily life. By watching us work with and for others, children can see how well we live up to the standards we set for the family. In our dining room we keep a pushka, a box, in which we put money for those in need. Before Alisa lights the Sabbath candles, each child deposits a coin in the box.

When children are still young, instead of just writing a check for a charity, we might set aside a special animal bank for each member of the family to put money in and then decide together when the bank fills up where the money should go. We might even encourage our kids to set aside a percentage of their allowance for a worthy cause or project that they decide on when the money accumulates.

Older children can come with us to visit someone in the hospital or help care for a family whose mother or father is ill. Visits like these will teach them something we already know: that they have the power to inspire and uplift other people's spirits and make them feel good. Children often don't realize how just their sheer presence can make someone they love feel better. We should give them every opportunity we can to learn this. Of course, we cannot be continually dragging children to do things for other people against their will, but even little gestures now and then can make them more sensitive to the good they can do. They will get first-hand experience at making the world a kinder and better place to live.

It's never too early to show a child that he or she lives in a bigger and more complex world than the family, but we should be careful not to overwhelm them with the injustice, violence, and terrorism that characterize so much of modern life. Children's imaginations are vivid and their nightmares can be terrifying. We shouldn't alarm them unduly about the tragedy of human life over which we have little or no control. A mother brought a five-year-old girl to my office who had become obsessed with death. The child was constantly asking how people were buried and what happened to them after they died. At one point she asked me what happened to the shovels that were used to dig the graves. I wasn't sure what she was getting at, but I told her they were put away until they were needed again. "You never put a shovel *into* the grave, do you?" she asked hesitantly. I told her no, we didn't. We talked some more and slowly it became clear that she really didn't have a morbid concern with death but was trying to handle a very sensitive fear. She had recently learned that Hitler had tried to kill all Jews and she was trying to reassure herself that he was really dead and there was no possibility he could dig himself out of the grave and return to threaten her.

Remember that children are not adults and we should not overburden them with activities, responsibilities, and adult problems that their experience and developing sense of rightness cannot yet handle. Be realistic in what you expect of them and forgive them when they don't live up to your expectations.

We cannot control every factor in our children's lives, nor should we want to, especially as they grow older. If we provide a loving but firm presence in their lives when they are young, they will most likely retain the core values we have tried to instill. During difficult periods when our children seem lost and confused, our presence and support can help them find their way. We can help them avoid the dead ends: preoccupations with alcohol, drugs, sex, money. Trying a drink and falling in love are normal rites of passage, but drug or alcohol abuse and reckless sexual activity are not prerequisites for becoming an adult. Peer pressure is only one reason a child engages in self-destructive behavior. It also takes parents who give up too easily, thinking that whatever they do just won't work.

Peers will always be an important influence on our children and will even help them develop an identity distinct from our own. We do not have to constantly criticize the values and lifestyles of our children's friends. If we stand up for our beliefs and make them an integral part of our daily living, our children will factor them into their own behavior along with the habits and ways of acting they pick up from their peers.

Our children may not always agree with us. They may not do what we want. They may ultimately choose to live by different values and standards, but in letting them know how we feel, we give them a model and a perspective with which to define their own conduct. A child who respects and trusts his parents will consider their expectations even when he argues vociferously and rebels against them.

A sixteen-year-old boy in my class astounded me with his conservative, traditional views about premarital sex and marrying only within the faith. He argued passionately and eloquently for couples not to live together before marriage and to marry only someone of their own religious convictions. Needless to say few students were on his side in the classroom debates. I know that at home the boy presents a different face to his parents. He calls them old fogies whenever they suggest the same values. He accuses them of being prejudiced against people of other faiths and out of touch with modern courtship practices. It will be interesting to see as the boy matures where his true sympathies lie.

The challenge of activist paraenting is to find the strength to love our children when they fight with us and with everyone around them. Can we love our children when they are homely, awkward, unkempt, flaunting the styles and friendships they know we don't approve of, when they fail to be the best, the brightest, the most accomplished at school or even at home? Can we be there when their world has fallen apart and only we can restore their faith and confidence in life?

Activist parenting is just as crucial to our children's development when they are in high school as when they were younger—perhaps even more so, now that they will come more solidly under the influence of their peers. They will need us to suggest limits and standards even if they cannot admit it. Under pressure to experiment with drugs or stay out late, it is often easier to say, "My parents won't let me stay," than to say, "I want to go home." They need us at home to listen and reassure them, to tell them they are attractive, competent, worthwhile human beings no matter what their friends say, or no matter what they think about themselves in their darker moments when they realize they have fallen short of even their own expectations. They need us to tell them after a lousy day that tomorrow will be better.

Raising a child toward menschlichkeit requires activist parents willing to always walk a tightrope between love and discipline, between praise and constructive criticism. We will make mistakes. Sometimes we will be too harsh, sometimes we will be too lenient. We cannot be too "fixed in our ways." As our children grow, we grow. No one has all the answers. I am sure that ten years from now I will be a different parent than I am today.

It will help us and our children if we can laugh at our faults. It will help us tolerate our shortcomings, and it will help our children see that the goal is to be a human, not perfect. My mother-in-law used to give evening lectures about books and often arrived home too late to tell her children how she did. So she would tape a self-evaluation to the refrigerator door for them to read in the morning. Sometimes it was in the form of a report card; sometimes it was simply a tally of how many people walked out and how many fell asleep. Her children learned that when things didn't go well, her whole world didn't collapse and neither would theirs. After all, we want our children to learn that we are human, like they are, and to learn that it's okay for them to be human just as we are. We are all lovable whether we are strong or weak, happy or sad, feeling on top of the world or down in the dumps. We want them to learn that through thick and thin we are all struggling to be menschen.

The goal of activist parenting is *makhn fun kinder menschen*, but it is a lifelong goal even for ourselves—for there is always a part of us that is less than perfect, that falls short of menschlichkeit and needs to be encouraged to keep trying. It is at once the most overwhelmingly frustrating and exasperating task and the most joyous and rewarding experience: to make human beings out of children.

5. If I'm O.K. and You're O.K., Then Our Child Is Not O.K.

He who instructs by personal example rather than mere words, his audience will take his counsel to heart. He who does not practice what he so eloquently preaches, his advice is rejected.

—COMMENTARY TO ETHICS OF THE FATHERS 3:9

When I was seven years old my mother took me with her to deliver a box of clothes to a family living in a small rural town in Central New Jersey where she taught kindergarten. After a ten-minute drive we arrived outside a long, low-roofed, weather-beaten building on the edge of a recently harvested field. The building had been partitioned into several compartments each of which housed a family. A door hung loosely on its hinges. In a dimly lit room with a dirt floor I saw three children and their parents. The oldest of the children, a boy about my age, ran to greet my mother and hugged her. His parents politely rose and said hello. There was little furniture in the room: a few beds shoved to one side, a wooden table, and a small stove. There was no sink or toilet. We spoke to the family for a half hour, and as we left my mother gave them the box of clothes. It was only thirty minutes of my childhood, but I remember the visit thirty years later as it if were yesterday.

Of the countless experiences of growing up, why do I still remember so vividly this visit to a migrant worker's family? Was it the shock that people lived in such poverty so close to us? Or an early feeling of guilt that other children had so few of the things I took for granted? Perhaps it was surprise that a child I had never seen had a relationship with my mother. I am sure it was a bit of all these things, but the central image of that day is my mother reaching out to help a family in need who clearly had nothing tangible to give in return.

We know that a child does not become a mensch merely because of the advice we give, the childrearing techniques we employ, or the pat formulas we read about in books. Moral sayings and proverbs do not guarantee menschlichkeit no matter how often we repeat them. Kindness is not taught by lecture or sermon. Kindness is a way of doing things learned in a family that does things in a kind way. Giving clothes to a migrant family was just one of the many kind things my mother did. And if our children are fortunate to know others outside the family—teachers, clergymen, scout leaders, camp counselors—who also act out of kindness and compassion, all the better.

A friend of mine remembers his eighteenth birthday quite clearly because as the youngest in a family of four boys, he had watched his father initiate each of his older brothers into adulthood on their eighteenth birthdays. He approached his eighteenth year with excitement and a little healthy apprehension. When the day arrived, his father took him to the local blood bank. Stretched out on tables beside each other, the father gave blood as he had done with each of his boys on their eighteenth birthdays while his youngest son gave blood for the first time in his life. To this day my friend feels compelled to give blood on the anniversary of his father's death and each time he lies there he recreates that special moment he shared with his father so many years ago.

That father is still a living example of menschlichkeit to his sons even though he has long passed away. Amidst all the hopes and dreams we have for our children, amidst all the compromises which life with other people necessitates, we hope that the important memories remain with them— memories of us living fully human lives of compassion and responsibility. We do not have to be remembered as perfect parents. "A mensch is only human," says a Yiddish proverb; and our children prefer it that way. Who wants saints and heroes for parents? I know a mother who is an attractive woman, always well-groomed, successful in her career, and utterly charming on every occasion. It's impossible to catch her off guard. Her fifteen-year-old daughter, with lank, dirty hair hanging over her face, dresses only in the sloppiest clothes, and barricades herself behind a glum exterior. Another mother told me half jokingly that she gained forty pounds during her daughter's adolescence so that the girl could rebel against her by remaining slim! It can be tough competing with a parent who is perfect.

Our children do not want models of perfection, neither do they want us to be buddies, friends, or confidants who never rise above their own levels of maturity and experience. We need to walk that middle ground between perfec-

tion and peerage, between intense meddling and apathy—
the middle ground where our values, standards, and expectations can be shared with our children. The very act of
bringing a child into the world has bestowed a responsibility and obligation on us which our children do not share or
totally understand yet. By the very fact that we are parents,
we owe them the wisdom of our years.

I often visit families mourning the death of a parent or
grandparent who was dearly loved. I've noticed over the
years that people do not dwell on what their parents or
grandparents did for a living, what kind of car they drove,
or how much they paid for their house. They talk of
menschlichkeit. Particularly in close families where the
lives of family members were intertwined, people tell me
of the small everyday gestures of love and kindness that
made a lasting impression. "Grandpa took me to the zoo on
Sundays." "Mom always waited for me at the bus stop so
that she could ask about my day." "Dad spent hours teaching me how to play checkers and then ignored all the strategies himself so that I could win." "One cold night I was
late from a date and Dad met me at the subway with his
overcoat over his pajamaas." These are the memories that
last. Long after a person's titles and professional accomplishments have been forgotten, the acts of menschlichkeit
remain.

A story in this vein is told about an extraordinary fundraiser in a little town in Poland. One evening the fundraiser
visited the son of a generous contributor who had recently
inherited his deceased father's wealth. The son was not
interested in contributing in the memory of his father and
asked the fundraiser to leave. "I am not interested in the
institutions which my father supported. Cross his name off

your list." "I am sorry," the fundraiser replied, "but I cannot do it. Your father put his name on my list, and only he can take it off. Since he is no longer here and you are his heir, you are the only one who has the right to cross off his name. Here is a pen. Strike out your father's name." The son took the pen; his hand started to shake. He knew he could not erase his father's name and obliterate his memory. In less dramatic ways, the power we exert over the future behavior of our children is enormous. Even after they have left home, even after we have left the world, there will always be part of us that will remain with them forever.

And yet outlooks do change with the passing of generations. The consensus of an earlier era that there was one right way of doing things has broken down. The popular self-help literature proclaims that one person's values or lifestyles are as good as another's so long as no one is hurt by our actions. The current wisdom asserts that "I'm O.K. and you're O.K." and everybody is O.K. But if all of us are O.K., then no one set of values or way of life is morally superior to any other. Perhaps well-meaning adults could live with this philosophy, but it raises a serious moral dilemma when we are forced to agree on what particular values to teach our children. Values become matters of personal likes and dislikes. Will we teach my values or yours? Do I have the right to impose my values on your children?

There are many reasons for this decline in consensus. In generations past the extended family lived either in the same house or nearby; and grandparents, aunts and uncles, cousins, all had a hand in raising and influencing the younger generation. My own family and relatives lived within a few blocks of one another and were always in one another's houses, consciously and unconsciously passing on a value system which spanned the generations. We lived and grew up in a community with a coherent set of values that impinged upon everyone's personal life. With less mobility, people knew one another over longer periods of time and became responsible and accountable to each other.

I still remember my grandparents' apartment building with the clotheslines strung across the back alley from their bedroom window to the next apartment house. The clotheslines were the telephone lines of their generation. Hanging out and bringing in the laundry was an occasion for passing the news from family to family. Sharing the daily struggles and triumphs of life with the neighbors was an everyday ritual. By evening the entire block knew that Uncle Joe was walking out again on Aunt Bea; Sam had landed a job that would finally make him rich; and David had proposed to Mildred who was still seeing Lenny.

The schools once reinforced common values, but rarely today is a school ranked by the moral values it teaches or the ethical stature of its students. When educators discuss values, they usually speak of "values clarification strategies" which assume that all values are relative and the important thing is not to know right from wrong but to understand the values you hold and why you hold them. The only point of agreement about what is wrong is that it's wrong for adults to teach a specific value system to children! Such strategies assume that values are already inside a child and simply need to be extracted by discussion and multiple-choice questions. A recent headline in the *New York Times* might have been concocted by Lewis Carrol to confuse Alice in her romp through Wonderland:

"Ethics Classes Avoid Teaching Right and Wrong."

Not only what they teach, but how teachers live is undergoing profound change. To suggest the traditional viewpoint that teachers should be held accountable as models for their students is to invite rebellion. A superintendant of a Massachusetts public school system thought he was simply stating the obvious when he wrote in the school's policy manual that instructors should behave morally and ethically in and out of school. He was met with a storm of protest from his staff and asked by the teachers' union to appear at a hearing in response to a complaint which they filed with the State Labor Relations Board. The teachers asserted that the superintendant had no right to arbitrarily dictate morals.

Religion, too, was once a powerful transmitter of values when the lives of most people centered more fully around synagogue and church. Religion provided a shared world view, with a common vocabulary enabling us to speak to one another about values and about God. It brought us together in common rituals that celebrated the fundamental beliefs that shaped our lives. It reminded us of our blessings and our obligations to help those who do not enjoy our good fortune. Religion defined right and wrong and grounded our assumptions in the absolute goodness of God.

When we begin to doubt the absolute goodness of God and even His very existence, we are left with only ourselves as the final arbiters of morality, and our all-too-human values reflect all the uncertainty that goes with living an all-too-human life. Our values become suspended within us, and reflect no broader sense of purpose than our own immediate concerns. We are no longer convinced that certain actions are objectively right or wrong for everyone. We replace the standard of what is right with the standard of what feels good. Instead of asking, "What is right, ethical, or moral?", we ask "How do I feel about that?", "Is it right for me?", and "How will it affect my life?" We look for values inside ourselves rather than from external sources. When values are no longer rooted in an absolute goodness, they become only as good as those who hold them; and even though we preach a democracy of ethical belief, we know intuitively that one person's goodness may not be as good as his or her neighbor's.

Values do not come from within; they come from without. Children need clearly defined values and standards against which they can test themselves. Morality is not only taught; it is caught. Young people acquire and form their own values and ideals by trying out the value systems to which they are exposed. No one ever became a mensch by sitting and meditating in isolation. The long discussions and painful arguments of adolescence and the fierce loyalties to teachers, heroes, and gurus during the teenage years are simply our children's struggles to ensure that the lifestyles and values they adopt are worthy of their allegiance.

When a young person finds no worthy tradition and no sensible values outside his or her own self, when our children test the world around them and nothing holds firm, they become premature cynics. Idealism dies. I sense that a generation or two ago young people had more heroes. I grew up hearing about the virtues of individuals such as Franklin Roosevelt, Harry Truman, Winston Churchill, Edward R. Murrow, and Joe DiMaggio. My own generation had John F. Kennedy, Golda Meir, Martin Luther King, Jr., Albert Einstein, and Bob Dylan. In the last two decades assassinations have dashed our hopes; political scandals have made us more cynical; and the media have poured salt on our wounds by debunking our heroes, exposing their private foibles, and highlighting every public failure.

A fourteen- or fifteen-year-old should be an idealist. If our son wants to become a doctor, part of his motivation should be to heal those in pain. If our daughter wants to become an attorney, she should be concerned about injustice. If our children want to become parents, they should have a desire to be better with their children than we were with them. There is plenty of time for the younger generation to learn that life with other people is a matter of compromise and accommodation and that no one is perfect. While they are still young, let's give them the ideals and values that will inspire them to reach beyond the merely reachable.

With the breakdown of the traditional institutions which convey values, more and more of the burdens and responsibility for transmitting values fall upon parental shoulders; and it is getting harder all the time both to embody the virtues we hope to teach our children and to find for ourselves the ideals and values that will give our own lives purpose and direction. We need a tradition and a community to support us, wherein being decent is given higher value than being best, where being good is more honored than being smart. We need a community that will defend our claims that values are not relative and that our responsibilities go beyond our own personal interests, a community that celebrates by ceremony and ritual the stages of life through which our children pass on their way to mature and responsible adulthood.

Within my own tradition I have often marveled at the transformation which a Bar or Bat Mitzvah can bring about in the life of a thirteen-year-old, who for the first time leads part of the service, shares in the religious honors reserved for adults, and speaks to all assembled about the significance of the occasion. Contrary to popular impression, the ceremony does not transform a thirteen-year-old into an adult overnight. After the Bar Mitzvah a parent still lives with an adolescent who has to be reminded to clean up his room, to do his homework, and to help around the house. At its best, however, the Bar Mitzvah demonstrates both to the thirteen-year-old and to all those present that a young person is growing toward adulthood and toward responsibility and obligations to a broader community.

There is nothing mysterious about how this happens. A public cermeony provides an occasion for a young man who often feels gawky and uncertain about himself to stand before a large group of people and demonstrate his competence by participating in the celebration and sharing in the religious honors and privileges reserved for adults. When I ask a boy after a ceremony how he feels, he usually just breathes a huge sigh of relief. When I catch him in a more reflective moment and ask what he learned about himself, the most common answer is, "I learned I could do it!" One girl told me that her Bat Mitzvah was an honor because people now saw her "on a higher level." All in all, the boy or girl confronts a task, masters the necessary skills, and demonstrates in a public context before a proud family that "I am no longer just a child."

There is much more to a Bar Mitzvah than the public ceremony. For most families, it is a gathering of friends and relatives. The front rows of the sanctuary are filled with the older and younger generations. The house teems with out-of-towners, and the thirteen-year-old never forgets relinquishing his room for the makeshift sleeping arrangements scattered around the house to accommodate everyone. Even if this is the only time the whole family gets together, the young generation is vividly reminded that it is tied to a family that is filled with grandparents, uncles, aunts, cousins, and in-laws.

When the festivities end and life gets back to normal, the honored child will sometimes tell me that he felt part of something beyond himself, a sense that he is linked to other generations besides his own, reaching deep into the collective past; and that he stands at a crucial moment in this chain of values and responsibilities, for he represents the present and the future, and upon him rest the choices that will determine whether the generations that follow will continue in the same tradition. He slowly realizes that he is not an isolated individual thrust into a meaningless world to make his lonely way. At a time in his life when he is bewildered and maybe even frightened by so many physical and emotional changes taking place within him, he feels connected to a stable tradition. As one boy put it:

> You feel that all your friends have done what you are doing. When you stand in front of everyone, you see all the earlier generations passing before you and know you are doing what they did when they were thirteen. And some day you know that your kids and their kids will do it too.

Every family needs occasions to join together publicly to rejoice, give thanks, and to mark the important points of transition in the lives of its members. Birthdays, weddings, graduations, and births are not just "one more day"—they are special and should be recognized as such. The crucial milestones in the lives of our children should not pass unnoticed. In fact, what we really take note of—and what they come to recognize in themselves—is their growth toward maturity and menschlichkeit.

To simply tell a son or daughter to show more responsibility is an impoverished statement compared to the effect of a ceremony which allows and encourages them to demonstrate that responsibility in the midst of a family, a community, and a time-honored tradition. Even if they don't feel overwhelmed by the significance of the occasion at the moment, they may look back years later and realize it was an important turning point in their lives. All family celebrations are important, but when they take place in a moral or religious context they acquire a special luster, reminding a child that morality is not simply a matter of personal preference nor of doing what he or she wants so long as it does not infringe upon others. Morality emerges from the obligations to yourself, to those around you, and to a broader community. It affirms that the central questions of life are fundamentally spiritual questions: "What is the right way to live? What is the decent thing to do?"—not "What's in it for me?"

Besides the cycle of life, we ought to celebrate the annual cycle of holidays and festivities both national and religious to deepen our sense of obligation to others. The warm rituals of our respective spiritual traditions remind us of the religious communities to which we are linked. The national holidays keep alive our commitment to the ideals of the country in which we live.

Within my own tradition Passover is a dramatic reenactment of the journey from slavery to freedom. We eat food that looks and tastes like that which was eaten by slaves. We sing songs that describe the oppression of slavery and express the gratefulness for being restored to freedom. We structure the ceremony to fire the imaginations of our children with questions and curiosity so they will ask what it felt like to be a slave and what it means to be free. Children who have never known hunger, suffering, or oppression reenact in myth and ritual the experience of being deprived of food and freedom.

If we can remember what it is like to be hungry and oppressed, we will sense more keenly our obligations to help those who, in our own day, suffer injustice and are treated cruelly by their fellow human beings, those who are alone or cast out, those reduced to poverty and starvation. With good reason the Passover celebration begins with an invitation to the poor and hungry to come into our homes: "Let those who are hungry enter and eat. Let those who are in need come and celebrate Passover." The Passover Seder is designed to make us remember the past and recognize our obligations to the present.

Of course a ceremony from any spiritual tradition can be drained of its power to remind and inspire when performed mechanically or by rote. At worst it becomes a meaningless or distorted formality, a hollow husk of what was once a rich and beautiful experience. It is easy to understand why children rebel against a ritual when it's imposed in a heavy-handed manner divorced from the values which nourish it. Yet at their best, rituals have the power and vitality to instill a sense of responsibility, compassion, and a shared life with others. They give our families warm and rich moments to come together and shape our family memories. A cookbook with great-grandmother's recipes hand-written in the margins, a wedding veil in which each bride of the family is married, a Bible handed down from generation to generation, inscribed with the family tree and taken to synagogue or church on special occasions, or, as in our own family, a white embroidered tablecloth used whenever the family marks a joyous milestone—these are the kinds of symbols and traditions that add depth to our lives and a connection to other generations.

I know it's difficult today in our mobile and impatient society to raise children in one particular tradition or community. We want our children to experience the best things that life has to offer and reap the benefits of living in a many-cultured land. Yet doing so entails risks. Several years ago Anne Roiphe published an article in the *New York Times* entitled "Christmas Comes to a Jewish Home," in which she described her Jewish family's celebration of a secularized version of Christmas. For Roiphe this was the inevitable and desirable consequence of American assimilation. Her children, she contended, were no longer mired in a "ghetto," but had friends from all backgrounds and identified with the universal aspirations of humanity and feminism.

The article was met by an onslaught of criticism, and after a great deal of soul searching, she wrote *Generation Without Memory* as a sequel to the article. In this book she questioned the wisdom of her assertion that you did not have to be rooted in a particular community or tradition. She recounts a parents' night shortly after her youngest daughter started kindergarten. One mother approached Roiphe and her husband and proudly pointed out her own daughter's sketch of a large Jewish star with a family of smiling stick figures underneath. The mother explained that family and Jewishness were central to her daughter's self-identity. Anne Roiphe then looked at her own daughter's picture, some blue and green colored smudges dripping into one another. Were these drippy smudges her daughter's sense of who she was? A month later Roiphe attempted to explain to her daughter that they were a family of humanists. The five-year-old's response was one of perplexed bewilderment. In conclusion Anne Roiphe wondered if by abandoning the beauty and mystery of a particular tradition, along with its moral commitment to past and future, she had in effect turned her family and herself adrift and anchorless on an uncharted sea. The universalism that had been her source of joy had now become her burden.

Neither we nor our children can identify with humanity at large. It is too impersonal an abstraction. Lovers of humanity are often intolerant of the individuals and groups that compose it. Some of the worst historical injustices have been perpetrated in the name of humanity. The Communist Revolution, for example, began with the noble ideal of ending economic oppression, but it gave birth to a regime that cruelly oppresses individuals and minorities who live under it.

Grounding our families in a religious or moral tradition, of course, is no panacea for all our problems, nor will it provide simple answers to the complexitites of life. The right and menschlich thing to do in any situation is not always clear. Many times we cannot determine which course of action is the right choice. How do we balance responsibilities that pull us in opposite directions? What should we do, for instance, when we are torn between the demands of aging and ill parents and the needs of our children? Who comes first, our children or our parents?

A mother recently came to me about the overwhelming responsibilities of caring for her frail, elderly parents who did not need a nursing home but clearly could not manage their apartment alone. In addition to hiring a housekeeper for them, the woman still had to make an hour's trip each day to help with the shopping and other household chores. A few months earlier her teenage daughter had exploded in fury about a dress her mother had promised to her and then had inadvertently forgotten while preoccupied with a minor crisis involving her own mother's medication. In the last month the teenager had grown depressed and withdrawn, apparently feeling guilty about the anger she harbored over her mother's neglect.

Clearly there were no easy answers. Fortunately, as we talked over the woman's options, we each understood the other because we shared the same references and spoke the same moral language. We were both rooted in a strong tradition of obligation and familial responsibilities. It made coming up with alternative plans much easier than if we had come from different backgrounds and spoke from conflicting sets of values. The solutions she came up with were not perfect but they were workable; and what's more, they were grounded in menschlichkeit. Whatever effect her plans would have on her family, she found great peace in knowing that she was operating from a strong moral center, shared by others in her immediate family as well as the generations who had gone before her.

For some of us it may not be easy to espouse a particular tradition or community because of differing religious or national backgrounds. For others of us a tradition and its rituals may seem outmoded and irrelevant to the way we live, the concepts and vocabulary as alien as a foreign language. We may have problems about God or have serious doubts about the moral practices and values of the religious institutions we were brought up in. Yet we would do well to try to overcome the doubts and obstacles that alienate us from a solid religious tradition. A sympathetic clergyman who can deal with our concerns without condemning us for our failures may be able to help.

Some of us may be reluctant to ground our children in a particular community or tradition because we want them to be free to choose their own beliefs and commitments and we erroneously believe that growing up in one community will prevent them from doing that. On the contrary, it will make whatever decision they make stronger and more purposeful. If they remain within a tradition, they are rooted in a rich network of family and community. If they search for another, at least they know what they are giving up. All decisions involve lost opportunities and roads not taken. When we teach our children one language, other languages cannot be their native tongue. By pursuing one profession, we miss out on another. And yet these choices are the only paths to accomplishment.

To be part of a tradition and community is the birthright of every child; it is the essence of our humanity. Children will not learn the standards and ideals we want them to have from television, the movies, or on the streets. Outside our home and religious institutions they are more likely to learn cynicism and despair rather than faith and hope. If we hope to create a world which our children can trust and a future in which they can believe, they need values which have withstood the test of time and standards against which they can measure their own emerging thoughts and feelings.

In the end there are no shortcuts or easy formulas for raising a mensch. We become menschen by living in a familial web of love and respect, reinforced by a spiritual tradition and a community that brings families together and reminds us of our obligations to one another.

I grew up in a college town. Often during the holidays my parents would invite students from the campus for dinner who lived too far away to go home. Years later when I, too, left home to live at school, I finally appreciated what it meant to share the holiday with a family rather than alone and away from home in an empty dormitory or apartment.

My wife recalls a childhood Passover the year the family invited a man who had just been released from prison after serving time for tax evasion. Shunned by his own family and a pariah in the community, the man had no place to go for the holiday. As Alisa's family retold the story of the exodus to freedom and sang the songs of the holiday, the man broke down in tears. A few days later he sent the following note: "I want to thank you for inviting me to your Seder. In this year when I have again become a free man, the celebration had a special meaning for me. Yet most of all I want to thank you for including me as part of your family. Your acceptance of me in your warm and close family made me feel like a human being again. May God bless you."

We may remember from our youth an act of generosity for those less fortunate, a holiday filled with song and rejoicing, a house bursting with happiness when the family was reunited for a joyous celebration. We remember them and we relive them. We carry these good memories in our hearts long after we cease to be children. These were the moments in which menschlichkeit was born; and whenever we recall them, we renew our commitment to those values so beautifully and vividly portrayed for us by our parents.

6. God: The First Mensch and Other Stories

> *Now the Lord has said, "Shall I hide from Abraham what I am about to do? . . . For I have singled him out, that he may instruct his children and his posterity to keep the way of the Lord by doing what is just and right. . . ."*
>
> —GENESIS 18:17, 19

Some of the first stories about menschlichkeit were composed thousands of years ago. Through the ages they have been passed down from generation to generation, until eventually they were collected in the book we call the Bible. Although terms like decency, compassion, fairness, and responsibility are never used, the message is clear: The early stories in Genesis are about menschlichkeit. They relate in dramatic detail how God and His creation struggle to learn ways of dealing with each other fairly and compassionately, each trying to live with the other. The first generations of men and women learn what responsibilities they owe to God and to one another. And even God Himself emerges as a mensch in His own dealings with human beings.

God is a mensch? Surely the characterization is a bit irreverent. A mensch is fully human; God is fully divine. But the early stories of the Bible show us how God becomes a model for human beings. He exemplifies the kindness, decency, and compassion that He hopes will characterize the way His children deal with one another. In doing so He does not diminish His own divinity; He increases His accessibility, making it easier for the first generations of human beings to imitate the qualities of menschlichkeit and create for themselves a society worthy of God's expectations.

The earliest stories in the Bible describe God struggling with His creation, adjusting His hopes and standards, coping with His disappointments and failures. In the beginning God starts out as do many parents, confident He has everything figured out. He assembles the world in six days without so much as a construction delay. Each aspect of the new world has its own day of creation. Adam, the first human being, is given all the advantages: a nice neighborhood, no crime, pollution, or rowdy neighbors, plenty of open space, natural food, and a pleasant job with eternal tenure. Adam will take care of the Garden, and God will take a sabbatical. The world is neat and tidy, except for one serpent.

So often new parents begin raising children with the same self-assurance. We put it all together: We know how many children we want, when we will have them, how much time we will take off from work, and how we will divide up childrearing responsibilities. Yes it doesn't take long to discover that children have minds of their own and that they aren't thinking along the same lines we are.

The first problem God faces is Adam's loneliness. All the advantages aren't enough for Adam. Adam is a social being as God Himself intended, but—was it an oversight? —He gave him no one with whom to socialize! It's the first hitch in creation, and God goes back to the drawing board. He matches Adam with all the animals, but nothing clicks. Adam names each animal but can find none to name "mate" or "companion." Finally God does a little reconstruction on one of Adam's ribs and fashions a woman. Instant success!

It's a remarkable story. God could have ignored Adam's loneliness. The world was a big place and presumably God had other interests and concerns beyond Adam. He could have outtalked Adam, convincing him that Eve wasn't in the original plan. Yet God sympathizes with Adam's loneliness and understands his predicament. The creation of Eve was a profound act of divine menschlichkeit.

The first problem solved, God still holds out for His much-earned sabbatical, but another unexpected turn of events interferes. He had given Adam and Eve one rule and it seemed so simple: Avoid that one tree. No curfews, no time clock to punch when tending the Garden, no fruit-picking quota. Only one requirement: Don't eat from the tree of knowledge.

Of course, Adam and Eve eat from it. Tell a child what not to do, and chances are he or she will just have to test it out anyway. Prohibitions create allurement. God had created Adam and Eve with free will and they decided to make the most of it, choosing and acting out of their desires, not God's.

God's predicament is a typical parental let-down. Our

children are fashioned in our own image and likeness, but the choices they make are not always our own. Like so many of us God would have preferred to give Adam and Eve the best of everything—material comforts, freedom from pain and suffering, a life without effort and toil—but he learns He cannot do it all for His children.

He informs the couple that their days of sheltered existence are over; it's time for the real world beyond the Garden. But God's banishment of Adam and Eve is not so much a punishment as it is a send-off to new possibilities, to a world that will stimulate creativity and pose a new reality. When He tells Eve that she will give birth to her own children in pain and Adam will earn his living by the sweat of his brow, God is describing the new world where struggle and choice will give grandeur and meaning to human life, previously unknown in the garden with its one simple rule. As a departing gesture of compassion, He clothes them with garments of skin, and sends them into a world blessed with His presence, but a world where they will succeed and fail on their own.

How easy it is for us as parents to say we want our children to grow and make their own choices. How hard it is to abide by those words when the choices they make are not ours. As they grow up, we urge them to become more independent, to fight their own battles, and stand on their own two feet; but we cry inwardly as they grow away from us and are wounded by life.

Even God finds it hard to come to terms with his struggling creation. In Noah's generation He lashes out against the wickedness that fills human society. Regretting His involvement with human beings who have made such a sorry state of the world and rebelled against His authority, He unleashes the flood. Surely we have all experienced such anger during periods in our children's lives when their every act displeases us and every choice seems wrong. Our pride turns to doubt, and we silently ask ourselves if the aggravation is worth it. Hopefully, those flashes of despair pass quickly and we go on. Yet it is never easy to accept that our children are not perfect versions of ourselves— that they too are people with weaknesses, limitations, and failures. The essence of menschlichkeit is our ability to accept our children as people in their own right and love them even when they disappoint us and make decisions we just don't understand or approve. Will we be able to find peace of mind when our children move far away from home, fail to continue the family business, or choose a way of life quite different from our own?

With Noah God acted like a parent who warns and dictates to a young child: I will send a flood; you will build a boat, get on board, save the animals! One, two, three! With Abraham we find God acting quite differently. We find a new mutuality. They confer with one another. God shares His intentions with Abraham, tests His ideas, runs His plans for Sodom and Gomorrah by him several times. He gives Abraham as much time as he needs to question His wisdom. In short, God treats Abraham as a partner in the divine plan to establish justice on earth. In dealing with Abraham God learns to fully accept the integrity, separateness, and maturity of a human being.

At the beginning of Genesis, we get the impression God could no more anticipate the difficulties to come from His creation than could a new parent looking for the first time into the innocent face of a newborn child. Tough moments lie ahead but we have few clues as to what they will be.

For God is was Adam's loneliness, the disobedience of the first couple, the destruction by the flood, the realization that He would have to change His approach in dealing with Abraham. Human parents, too, truly hoping to live in His image, will have to learn to respect the dignity and sacredness of others.

As the Bible stories unfold, we meet men and women who struggle in their own ways to imitate God's menschlichkeit. They live before God and within their families, and exercise their responsibilities and obligations in the day to day ambiguities of human life. They are not perfect people. Sometimes they build on the achievements of generations that have gone before; sometimes they slip back. At times they live up to God's expectations; at times they falter. We see them honestly confronting the divine imperatives of human life, but we also see them running away from God, seeking to evade Him. They are strong and weak, kind and cruel; they hurt and cause pain to others, frequently the ones they love the most. They are people like us.

Yet the measure of their lives is never based on what they produce, what they look like, or how useful they are. They are not measured by I.Q. scores, S.A.T. tests, college degrees, psychological profiles, or annual salaries. The measure of their lives is their ability to live responsibly in the world God has given them and to respond compassionately to the human problems they confront. Except for occasional moments of anger and weakness, they know they are responsible to God, created in His image and called to respect the community of living things to which they belong. When they are callous or irresponsible, they feel God's anger and disappointment. When they carry out

His will, they walk in God's footsteps, and they know they have acted as menschen.

Each generation in Genesis struggles with its divinely appointed destiny, often within the intense emotional bonds of the family where strong feelings of love can turn to passionate hate, and the blood connection of brothers can erupt in fraternal jealousy and envy. In the early Biblical stories we find such a series of brothers struggling toward menschlichkeit. In their moments of weakness and triumph, we can see our own successes and failures.

The first pair of brothers is Cain and Abel. We know little about them. Cain offers God the fruits of his harvest; Abel sacrifices a lamb from his flocks. For some reason— God chooses not to tell us—Abel's offering is accepted and Cain's is not. We know that Cain is devastated and, lashing out in rage, kills his brother. When Cain replies to God's question, "Where is your brother Abel?", with "Am I my brother's keeper?", he shrugs off any responsibility for his brother and violates the fundamental principle of interdependence upon which God has established the world. God condemns Cain to a lonely life of ceaseless wandering over the face of the earth.

The next pair of brothers we meet are the half brothers, Ishmael and Isaac, sons of Abraham. Isaac was born of Abraham's wife, Sarah, and Ishmael of Sarah's handmaid, Hagar. One day Sarah demands that Abraham cast Ishmael and his mother out of the house. We can only surmise her intention. Could she not bear the thought that her own son would develop a friendship with the son of her handmaid? Did Ishmael's presence remind Sarah that in a moment of despair she had consented to let her husband have a child by her handmaid? Is she worried Ishmael will demand a stake in Isaac's inheritance? The brothers are separated and grow up apart from one another, each to live his own life. Only when their father Abraham dies do the two brothers come together briefly to mourn his passing.

In the next generation, the twin sons of Isaac do not make an auspicious entrance into the world. They fight while still in the womb. At birth Jacob emerges grabbing Esau's heel, already striving to overtake him. Never was there a clearer case of inborn rivalry! Jacob, the more subtle, knows how to manipulate his older brother, Esau. He tricks Esau in a moment of hunger to sell his birthright for a pot of stew. Then, disguised as Esau, Jacob tricks their father into giving him the more favored blessing belonging to the older son. Esau's initial reaction is to try to kill Jacob, but the deceiver flees, and for twenty years the two brothers dwell apart. Years later Jacob initiates a reconciliation and they seem to be reunited. Still the years of estrangement and suspicion cannot be entirely overcome. Distrust lingers, and the two brothers return to their separate homes.

Among the last generation of brothers in Genesis is Joseph, a spoiled and somewhat arrogant young man, who brings bad reports about his ten other brothers to his father, Jacob. Spurned by his older brothers, Joseph retreats into an active dream-life where he compensates for his outcast status with visions of his brothers someday bowing down before him to pay homage. To compound matters, he boasts about his dreams to his family! Fed up with his arrogance, the brothers cast Joseph into a pit and leave him for slave traders or death. Jacob, their father, is a broken man over his favorite son's disappearance.

The story moves on to Egypt where Joseph rises from

slavery to second in command under Pharoah. Famine in Israel forces the older brothers to journey in search of grain to Egypt, where, unbeknownst to them, their scorned brother is in charge of food rationing. To test their loyalty, he plants his silver goblet in the sack of grain given to Benjamin, the youngest and now favorite son. Later Benjamin is accused of stealing the goblet, and Joseph demands that he remain as his slave. In doing so, Joseph has set up his brothers to replay the incident in which they had abandoned him many years before. Would they still harbor feelings of resentment and once again abandon the youngest son?

To Joseph's surprise, the brothers stand by Benjamin. In an eloquent speech Judah defends the brothers' responsibility to Benjamin and to their father. In fact, the favored love of their father for their younger brother, once the cause of their cruelty toward Joseph, is now Judah's strongest defense. Leaving Benjamin in slavery in Egypt would send their father to his death. In an act of family loyalty Judah offers to remain as a slave in place of Benjamin. The love and allegiance that has developed among his brothers is too much for Joseph to bear. In tears he reveals his identity and invites his father along with all his brothers and their families to Egypt where they can live prosperously under his protection. Joseph, foreswearing vengeance, declares he has found purpose in his life by saving the Egyptians and his family from starvation and by forgiving his repentant brothers.

The human family has progressed a great distance from the first generation in Genesis until the last. In these struggles between brother and brother, we find each generation drawing closer to the model of menschlichkeit God has set before them. From Cain who repudiates all responsibility for Abel to Judah who would trade his own life for Benjamin's, we witness a hard and painful process of brothers learning to treat one another with decency and mutual respect.

God demands an ethical standard of behavior, modeled on the obligations and responsibilities which He himself has accepted toward His creation. Some of the Biblical characters succeed, some fail, usually it is a little of both. But precisely because God Himself emerges as a mensch, the Biblical families have a model for ethical behavior, a divine model of justice and kindness yet accessible to human understanding.

If we can read the Bible with an open mind and not dismiss it as an irrelevant relic, it can help us define our personal values and our responsibilities toward others, especially our children who are made in both God's image and our own. As God declared at the outset of creation, "It is not good for man to be alone." Relationship is at the core of human life, even as it is at the core of our human connection to God. Being human means being for others. Adam cannot live without Eve. Cain cannot live without Abel. A brother looks out for his brothers. The yardstick of our humanity is how we live with and for others.

These Biblical stories can help our children define their values and ideals. For younger children the stories need to be retold and simplified. Isaac B. Singer's *Why Noah Chose the Dove*, Marilyn Hirsh's *Tower of Babel*, and Lillian Freehof's *Stories of King David* and *Stories of King Solomon* are written in readable English while retaining the power and charm of the original.

While the Bible is perhaps the most comprehensive portrait of a world of meaning and enduring value, many wonderful books can inspire our children to live lives of menschlichkeit. A few of our favorites from among hundreds include: Barbara Cohen's *Molly Pilgrim*, the story of schoolchildren who learn to respect an immigrant girl and her customs; Florence Freedman's and Robert Parker's *The Brothers*, an ancient legend about two brothers who each shares his wealth with the other, assuming the other is in greater need; Vera Williams' *A Chair for My Mother*, about a family that saves its pennies to buy a chair for mama so she can put her feet up after a hard day's work; Dare Wright's *Edith and Mr. Bear*, the story of a girl who lies about breaking a clock and learns after a great deal of pain and loneliness that it is better to take responsibility for what you have done; the entire series of books by James Marshall about George and Martha, two hippopatamuses who always try to work out day-to-day relationships with each other in a loving and caring way; any book by Charlotte Zolotow or Franz Brandenberg.

For older children, the *Diary of Anne Frank*, *A Christmas Carol*, *King Lear*, and Martin Luther King's *Why We Can't Wait* are powerful narrations about the corrosive effects of indifference and the redeeming possibilities of understanding and kindness.

A good book can remind children that they are not alone as they struggle to grow up. Books such as Judy Blume's *Subterfuge* and *Tales of a Fourth Grade Nothing*, Barthe DeClements' *Nothing's Fair in Fifth Grade*, and Beverly Cleary's *Ramona and Beezus* series remind a child that everyone has trouble getting along with parents, brothers and sisters, and friends.

The best stories last far longer than the toys, trinkets,

and Transformers that soon break and are cast aside, having ceased to hold a child's interest. Even when the books themselves wear out, children forever keep in their imaginations a favorite tale which inspires their idealism and warms their hearts.

The real importance of books is not that they build vocabulary or raise reading levels. Their beauty is the presentation of purer and more consistent ideals than we can ever offer as parents. A good book shows children that the world is a good place containing admirable and humane individuals, that companionship, justice, and respect for others are possible. The best books anchor children in the moral tradition of their culture.

Children are entitled to a childhood. They will learn soon enough that there are some situations in which they will have to compromise their ideals. But before the realities of adulthood descend upon them, we owe it to them as their parents to fill their hearts and minds with the promise of a better world based on hope and human kindness.

After reading the story of Joseph and the famine, my daughter Ilana asked how much money would be needed to make all the poor people in the world rich. Her comment reflected a simplified view of world poverty, but it showed the power of the classic tale to trigger feelings of compassion and dreams of making the world a better place. Each year a busload of schoolchildren from our community participates in the annual march in New York City to show support for Russian Jews behind the Iron Curtain. To prepare them we read and discuss some of the Biblical stories in which people rescued their brothers and sisters from captivity. They learn about our obligations to others in the human family, and even more, they learn that *they* can make a difference. The year Anatoly Shcharansky, a leading Soviet refusenik, was freed, a seven-year-old student in the march told me, "I helped free Shcharansky."

A good book by itself will not make a mensch. Even "The Good Book" alone will not instill the qualities of menschlichkeit. The lessons of good literature must not remain between the covers of books, but be lived out in daily life where our children can see them and imitate them. With compassionate and firm parenting, we can teach our children their responsibilities to one another and to God.

7. *Be a Mensch*

*Vu es zaynen nit keyn menschen, say du a
mensch*—In a place where there are no menschen,
be a mensch. ·

—YIDDISH SAYING BASED ON ETHICS OF THE FATHERS 2:5

Is raising a child to be a mensch really in the child's best
interests? It would appear not. From popular folk wisdom
which asserts "Nice guys finish last," to the writings of
Freud which depict the individual as an aggressive creature
seeking to gratify instincts toward wealth, power, and success, to Desmond Morris's *Naked Ape* which suggests
human beings are and always have been predators, there is
a large body of literature telling us in no uncertain terms
that we should look out for ourselves before we look out
for others. Even altruism is defined by many modern psychologists as a selfish act which some self-deceiving people engage in because it makes them feel good—as if an
act that brings pleasure is only performed for the selfish
purpose of getting a kick out of it! Is altruism only the old
wolf of selfishness dressed in sheep's clothing?

Should we sympathize with the young man who complained to his father, "I'm tired of being good. All my life you told me if I was good, I would succeed. Why should I try to be a mensch when twenty of the most successful people I know are cheats and scoundrels?" Do we really have faith in the young man's father who replied, "I am sure your list contains twenty successful crooks, but if you look further you will find twenty others who are successful and good"?

We all trudge through life with a lot of cultural baggage packed with both streetwise aphorisms and scholarly analyses about the inherent evil in human nature. At times we feel like we are running against the grain in trying to be good. It's certainly more gratifying to measure ourselves against the world's criminals rather than the world's saints because we come out looking so much better! If we convince ourselves it's really not possible, or even psychologically healthy, to be a mensch, it's much easier to rationalize our shortcomings and justify our inadequacies.

It is no wonder that we are at best mistrustful of being good and, at worst, cynical about the possibility. Menschlichkeit is like love—it makes us vulnerable. It can set us up to get hurt. Kindness is not always returned. A friendly hello can be met with stony silence. A hand extended in welcome may be ignored. An offer to help may be refused. The people we love will sometimes reject us.

We know that it is a tough, demanding world in which nice guys often get stepped on. I'm sure you can remember an occasion when your act of decency was mistaken for weakness, or when you got stuck with some thankless job or assignment because you tried to be helpful. We have a right to ask ourselves if we are preparing our children for real life by teaching them to act fairly and decently at all times. Or are we creating social outcasts by raising them to value integrity in a world that often rewards expediency?

I believe that menschlichkeit carries its own rewards. More often than not our kindness is appreciated. A compliment truly makes a friend's day or even his whole week. A few minutes to listen reminds our spouses how much we care. An arm around our children's shoulders reassures them that we have confidence in them. What we give will usually be returned in trust, warmth, and love.

Menschlichkeit is not the same as soft-headedness, indecision, or weakness. A mensch is not a fool. To be a mensch we do not have to overlook the presence of evil. Being a mensch does not mean passive acquiescence. Yiddish has a different word for the person who is ignored and pitied for weakness and innocence—nebbish.

A mensch is not a nebbish. Evil is real, and menschlichkeit demands a self-confidence and strength of character to resist it. In a world where doing the moral thing is not always the popular path to follow, menschlichkeit demands the backbone to say no as often as it entails the nerve to say yes, to make hard decisions and stand firm. A mensch knows when compromise is the fairest solution to a problem and when strict adherence to principle is necessary to ensure justice. The world we live in is more challenging than the Garden of Eden because there are never perfect choices and only a range of imperfect possibilities. A menschlich way of life encompasses the intelligence and clearheadedness to find solutions that cause a minimum of pain, hurt, and injustice.

Friends of ours recently tried to keep their fourteen-year-old son, Michael, from going to an unchaperoned party that they strongly suspected would include drinking and drugs. The boy protested and promised he would not do anything wrong and his parents should trust him. Reading between the lines, our friends realized that this was the first time Michael had been invited to a party by the "in" group at school, and it meant a great deal to him to go and feel accepted. So they allowed him to go. When he came home later the night of the party, they asked him how it went. Michael told them matter-of-factly that there was so much beer drinking going on that it ruined the party and he had spent most of the time upstairs chatting with the host's parents who were home after all. Our friends were greatly relieved to learn how level-headed Michael had been and that by compromising their rule about no parties that involved drink or drugs, they had given their son the chance to learn that the social group he was so anxious to join was, in fact, as he put it, "pretty dumb."

We gain in our authority as parents when we are menschen, when we are sensitive enough to distinguish when it is necessary to hold fast and when to bend, when to speak out and when to hold our tongues. There is a moral authority which comes with doing the right and decent thing. As we learn that, perhaps our children will learn it too.

A mensch does not finish last. People are desperately seeking individuals whom they can rely on, who accept responsibility and make decisions based on fairness and compassion. In a time when few heroes remain untarnished, we look for decent people we can admire and respect. A mensch never loses the race; in fact men and women who are menschen are the few people who can look back upon their lives knowing they have lived the way they should. They can grow old at peace with their consciences;

and when life draws to a close, they know they have finished first among those who know and love them.

And while a mensch is victorious, he does not measure his success by fame, fortune, or power. The true reward of menschlichkeit is not any tangible compensation or human acclaim, but simply knowing we have done the right thing. Every family, career, and profession has room and reward for a mensch. The young man who found only cruel and ruthless people at the top wasn't looking very hard. It is not just the heartless who are successful. In every organization and type of work you'll find decent people who also rose to the top. A fundamental kindness and fairness runs through everything they do. They are a joy to know and work with. Those who feel they have to play "hardball" in their professions often leave injured feelings and disrupted lives in their wake. If they bring their tough attitude home, they often ruin their marriages and alienate their children.

A young man once asked me for advice about whether to become a doctor or not. He had just graduated from college and had always dreamed of entering medicine, but he had a very poor image of the medical profession. He didn't want to become "a pill-pushing, patient-counting, fee-collecting doctor who would never have time to hug or play with a child." I had a more positive image of the medical profession than this young man, but nothing would shake his negative perception. He went off to medical school with a strong conviction that I was wrong and he was right. Today he is still rather intolerant of the profession and refuses to enter private practice. But his love for medicine has led him to do research on childhood diseases, and thus he has found a way of remaining loyal to his principles while using his talents.

A mensch is a mensch for all seasons. There is no such thing as a fair-weather mensch. In Yiddish there is a revealing expression: "A mensch is always a mensch." The quality of menschlichkeit is so fundamental to a person's character that decency and fairness are a part of everything he or she does. It is a basic orientation to life, a way of being in the world, a way of living before God. A mensch is not one way in public and another way in private, one person in the street, a different person at home. He does not say nice things in the presence of people and then gossip about them behind their backs. A mensch is decent and responsible in all his or her relationships. The truest indicator of menschlichkeit is how we live among the people we love the most and can so easily take for granted. In some ways it is easier to be civil and respectable with friends and professional acquaintances than in the privacy and intimacy of our families. My wife often comments that what she loves most about her father, a rabbi, is that he is the same compassionate man off the pulpit as on it.

Menschlichkeit requires no heroic actions, professional training, or innate talents. It emerges in the smallest details of our lives: running down the street behind a son learning to ride a bicycle; helping a daughter master fractions; holding the hand of a sleepless three-year-old scared of wicked witches and monsters; consoling a daughter who has broken up with her first boyfriend; listening patiently to a child calling long distance from college because he needs to be reassured that his parents love him and that he still can come home.

A mensch is not a martyr, but simply a person who seasons the small gestures of everyday life with consideration, concern, and respect for everyone with whom he or she deals. Most people are decent to someone from whom they want help, friendship, sex, or a promotion. A mensch treats everyone decently, from the office subordinate with no political clout to the stranger who asks for directions. When the man who served as the White House stenographer for thirty years recently retired, he was asked which president he enjoyed working for the most. He replied that Harry Truman had been his favorite because he was the only president who had called him by his name.

Menschlichkeit is the most democratic of all values. There is no aristocracy of kindness or decency. A person is judged on kindness and compassion, qualities that know no social bounds, are not restricted by economic status, age, or gender. You cannot buy your way into the ranks of menschen. It does not automatically come with age, nor is it the prerogative of one sex over the other. There are young people who are kind and old people who are cruel, men who are compassionate and women who are heartless.

Menschlichkeit is available to everyone. It can be cultivated and nurtured. As parents we must believe that our children will want to model themselves after our example and that we can draw out the best in them. Even more so, we must be convinced that there is no more worthy ideal or legacy we can leave them. Be honest and forthright with them. Hug them when they make you proud. Correct them when they have been cruel or indifferent. Listen to their worries and remind them of their strengths. Forgive them when they need another chance and help them start again.

If there is one point about raising children to be menschen that you must believe and practice with all your heart it is to trust yourself. Believe in your natural ability to be a parent. Listen once again to the quiet counsel of your inner voice and the gentle promptings of your heart. We know more about being parents than others would have us believe. We should not be always worried about meeting an expert's standard. Menschlichkeit belongs to us, not the experts. It grows and develops in the common sense and natural love we have for our children.

When life is stormy, remember the story of Eleazer Hull, a New England sea captain who had no training in navigation but was hired by merchants throughout the Northeast. Once when Hull was asked how he steered his ships with such a sure hand through the hazards and unknowns of the seas, he replied, "I go up on the deck, listen to the wind in the rigging, get a drift of the sea, gaze at a star, and set my course." One year the State Commissioner of Navigation discovered that Hull was unlicensed and untrained in the science of navigation and told him he would have to get an education and upgrade his skills. Hull consented, graduated at the top of his class, received a certificate of achievement, and was told he was now licensed to return to sea. He did so, and when he returned from his first two-year-long voyage, his friends asked him how it felt to sail by the new scientific principles he had learned from books. Hull replied, "Whenever I needed to chart my course I pulled out my maps, followed the equations, and calculated my location with mathematical precision. Then I went up on the deck, listened to the wind in the rigging, got the drift of the sea, gazed at a star, and corrected my computations."

If we as parents keep a steady gaze on what is decent and good—if we let our natural instincts be guided by our experience and a moral tradition that can sort out our confusion and harness the darker sides of ourselves—if we do not let the advice of the experts drown us in insecurity, ignorance, or cynicism, we can raise children who will steer their own decent courses through life.

Even with common sense and a strong tradition behind us, we will still make mistakes. Neither you nor I can be the perfect parent any more than our offspring can be perfect children. Fortunately children are resilient. We can all look back at particular times and say that we could have handled them better. On any given day we may have said words we regretted or responded too curtly, lost our temper, or let a little one cry too long before we came to pick him up. Children recover. They are not formed or molded by the lack of a hug here or a few harsh words there. Only an ongoing pattern of neglect and abuse will permanently misshape their lives.

There will be especially difficult periods when we wonder if our kids will ever grow into mature adults. Physically they always grow taller; emotionally they sometimes grow smaller. One day they act like young adults; the next they pick a fight with a brother or sister befitting a two-year-old. The emotional and moral growth of our children is never a smooth progression from immaturity to responsible adulthood. Children will always need to test the limits, do something wrong, experiment with forbidden behavior, rebel over dress, drinking, or dating—do what they know gets our goat! None of this necessarily foreshadows an irresponsible adult. If we can avoid despair and self-doubt during the difficult periods and acknowledge our children's growth and accomplishments during the good ones, we will be able to hold onto our hopes that our kids will grow up into kind and considerate adults.

In the end we should remember that we do not strive to

be decent and responsible adults only for the sake of our children. We are trying to be more than just examples of menschlichkeit. We are trying to be actual menschen. Why? Because it is the right way to live. Even if our children should someday disappoint us with their way of life, we know that we have chosen to live justly.

An old legend recounts the attempt of a righteous man to learn the secrets of the world to come. God granted his wish and sent a heavenly guide to escort him to hell whereupon they entered a large room of a splendid palace. The residents of hell were seated around a banquet table laden with mouth-watering food and every imaginable delicacy piled high on golden platters. But nothing had been touched. The emaciated dinner guests moaned constantly in hunger and pain. The visitor asked his guide why, if they were hungry, they didn't eat. "Look closely," the guide replied as he pointed at them. "They have no elbows and their arms are locked straight before them. They cannot bend their arms to bring the food to their mouths."

The divine emissary then took his visitor to heaven where they entered a lavish banquet room identical to the one in hell—the diners had the same locked-elbow condition that prevented them from bending their arms to bring food to their mouths. Yet here everyone was well fed and joyous. "What gives?" the visitor asked his guide. "Why are these people so content if they too cannot help themselves to the food?" The heavenly guide told the man to look more closely. He did and discovered that each person lifted his or her stiff unbending arms to offer food to the person across the table.

Hell's torture is the absence of menschlichkeit; heaven's joy, its presence. Sartre claimed that hell was other people, but he was only partially correct. It is unmenschlich people—selfish, self-centered, uncaring individuals condemned to live in eternity the way they lived on earth and in the company of others just like themselves.

There is a Yiddish saying: "A mountain cannot meet a mountain but one person can reach out to another." Speak kindly of others. Tell a colleague it was a job well done. Remind a friend you value their companionship and help. Reassure your spouse and children that you love and need them.

Our most important task as parents is raising children who will be decent, responsible, and caring people devoted to making this world a more just and compassionate place. We *can* fashion for ourselves and our children a warmer, kinder world that will dispel the darkness and isolation. A life of menschlichkeit leaves a legacy for our children that will inspire them long after we are gone. When God measures us at the end of our days, He will put the tape around our hearts, not our heads.

It has been many years since I was a child, but in my own heart I continue to hear the question asked so often in my youth by my own father and mother. When I speak too quickly, when I turn a deaf ear to a friend, when I am insensitive to my wife or impatient with my children, the haunting question from my childhood continues to be the touchstone of everything I do. "When will you become a mensch?"

About the Author

NEIL KURSHAN currently serves as the rabbi of the Huntington Jewish Center in Huntington, New York. He is a Phi Beta Kappa graduate of Princeton University and received his Ph.D. in education from Harvard University. He was ordained a rabbi by the Jewish Theological Seminary. He has taught both in public and private schools and is rearing four children.